2/18

SURVIVING BERLIN

SURVIVING BERLIN

AN ORAL HISTORY

Karl M. von der Heyden

MCP Books
2301 Lucien Way #415
Maitland, FL 32751
407·339·4217
www.MCPBooks.com

Brandenburg Gate, May 1945 (Cover): Image ID: DKYTEA, dpa picture alliance/Alamy Stock Photo; Map of Europe 1922: Department of Military Art and Engineering, US Military Academy; WWII one-man roadside air raid shelter: Das Archiv für technische Dokumente 1900-1945, Wikimedia Commons; Bombed-out Berlin: Image ID: E14N8H, Keystone Pictures USA/Alamy Stock Photo; Map of Berlin Airlift Corridors: Free Software Foundation, Wikimedia Commons; British Sunderland seaplane: Image ID: CNRHPT, CPC Collection/Alamy Stock Photo; Gail Halvorsen: US Air Force, Wikimedia Commons; MS *Italia*, 1957: postcard courtesy of author; Lido Beach Hotel: postcard courtesy of author.

ISBN-13: 978-1-63505-614-3

Distributed by Itasca Books

Printed in the United States of America

CONTENTS

FOREWORD

Norman Pearlstine

Every profession has its Babe Ruth or its Duke Ellington—a legend whose career defies comparison. Every successful enterprise has its secret weapon—that trusted individual who gets results while shunning the limelight.

Karl von der Heyden is both.

Between 1980 and 2001 he served as the CFO of three of America's largest consumer products companies: HJ Heinz, RJR Nabisco, and PepsiCo. In those jobs Karl was more than the numbers guy. He was also the consummate dealmaker, very much responsible for each of the companies' mergers and acquisitions. He supervised complex corporate restructurings. And he was the straight shooter, often telling CEOs what they might not want to hear. He did so in ways that changed behavior and beliefs. No wonder he became a trusted advisor to CEOs elsewhere, who routinely sought his guidance. Many asked him to join their boards and he served as an independent director on a dozen large publicly held companies, including the New York Stock Exchange (later NYSE Euronext), DreamWorks Animation, and Macy's.

It is hard to think of other American executives who matched Karl's accomplishments. And none of them possessed his self-effacing nature.

Surviving Berlin is Karl's story. It begins with his birth in Berlin in 1936, followed by his poignant recollections of growing up in Nazi Germany. Following the war Karl's family remained in West Berlin during the

Occupation, experiencing constant hunger, as did so many other Germans. He came to America in 1957 to attend Duke University before embarking on his business career.

Along the way he became an American citizen. But it is those years in Germany that best explain his subsequent success and his admirable demeanor. While at Duke, he says he searched through old newspapers "trying to figure out how mass murder on the grandest scale by a great civilized society could have been perpetrated." And even today Karl says he is "part of a generation of Germans plagued by guilt about what the Nazis did" to Jews and other minorities.

Those early years also help explain Karl's lifelong commitment to philanthropy. He and his wife, Mary Ellen von der Heyden, have funded numerous fellowships and an addition to the library at Duke; they also helped build a new arts center there.

I came to know Karl in recent years when he served as chairman of the American Academy in Berlin while I was its president. Applying his financial skills to the Academy, he more than tripled its endowment, and he and Mary Ellen also endowed a fellowship for fiction.

Despite his obvious talent for business, Karl tells me he grew up wanting to be a journalist—and that he somehow got sidetracked along the way. I am so pleased that with *Surviving Berlin* he has begun to pursue his true calling.

Karl writes that his background taught him to be "skeptical of extremists, be they political ideologues or religious fanatics" and that he shudders "at the expression of too much overt patriotism, flag waving, or talk of 'exceptionalism' of this or that country."

I can only hope he will continue to write and that he will further enlighten us as he discovers more about himself and the world he and we live in.

PREFACE

Many people have urged me to write down the story of my life. After all, I witnessed some of the major turning points of the twentieth century. But, truth be told, I never had a particular interest in talking about any of it, including my upbringing in Germany during World War II.

But, with the help of Marc Rosenwasser, an award-winning journalist and television producer, I began to recall my life in bits and pieces. Over the course of a year and a half, we sat in my study and talked at great length. Each step of the way, he prodded me to remember, to mine the truth. While I supplied the vodka and dark chocolates, he supplied the questions.

Memories are, at best, capricious. Some of my recollections are second hand: what, for example, I heard as a child from my mother or other adults, from my late brother (who was seven years older than I), or from the newspapers and radio broadcasts. To make sure I got it right, I am indebted to my wife, Mary Ellen, and my older sister, Gisela, both of whom offer their own accounts herein, sometimes filling in the gaps, sometimes serving as gentle corrections. Their recollections are italicized wherever they appear. As you'll read briefly later, my wife also got involved in a very personal way during the Cold War.

The events described in this book cover a period of a little more than a quarter century—from the summer of 1936 until the summer of 1963: the first third of my life. During that time, Hitler, who ruled over Nazi Germany from an office maybe ten miles from my home, carried out the mass extermination of six million Jews. When the Allies finally defeated Nazism, World War II gave way to the Cold War and the rise of Communism. My hometown, Berlin, was—for forty-five years—the potential flashpoint between East and West. During this same period, race relations here in America went through a major upheaval, with segregation finally giving way to the beginnings of integration. Through happenstance, as much as anything else, I witnessed it all close up—first in Berlin, then in the southern United States.

I was born in the summer of 1936 in Berlin—the heart of Nazi Germany. From the time I was three until I was nearly nine, my life was shaped by the war raging above and around me. Although I was only a young child, I was keenly aware of my surroundings. As with so many children who have lived through violent conflict, I grew up fast. Though my parents did all they could to keep me out of harm's way, the war took an unmistakable toll: first, with disruptions to our daily lives; and, later, with massive destruction and deprivation, which I both witnessed and experienced. In the years following the war, my family and I, like millions of other Germans, personally experienced constant hunger.

For many years after peace came to Germany, the consequences of that horrific war continued to define my everyday existence. I spent a great deal of time during my years at Duke University in the late 1950s and early 1960s poring over old newspapers, trying to piece together what the Nazis did, trying to understand what my own parents knew, trying to figure out how mass murder on the grandest scale by a great civilized society could have been perpetrated. Even today, seven decades later, I am part of a generation of Germans plagued by guilt about what the Nazis did to the millions of Jews and other minorities they somehow deemed inferior. I am ashamed to be associated in any way with the greatest holocaust in history.

In no way is anything in this memoir meant to compare my family's travails with the terrible suffering experienced by so many during and after the war. There is no comparison of any kind to be made.

PREFACE

This memoir is only meant to fill in some blanks about what life was like in Germany during and after the war years and how one German came to learn about, visit, and ultimately embrace America, a country I am now a citizen of—a country I love.

The United States has been very good to me. Thanks to an abundance of luck, a solid education in Germany and later at Duke and Wharton, and some decent business skills, I forged a successful business career in the United States.

My journey from the bomb shelter outside my childhood home in Germany to the corporate boardrooms in America is definitely an unlikely one.

But ultimately, mine is a story of good fortune. After all, the very title of this book is *Surviving Berlin*.

PART I
GERMANY

ONE

THE WORLD I WAS BORN INTO

1936 was a big year for Berlin, my hometown. The Olympic Games had been awarded to the city, and Hitler pulled out all the stops to make the Games a propaganda success for the Nazi regime. He wanted to show the world a peaceful Germany and even temporarily suspended persecution of Jews and other minorities. He largely succeeded in his effort to fool an uncritical world.

That's the world I was born into, on the eighteenth of July 1936, in a women's clinic in the district of Wilmersdorf. I caused trouble right away. My parents had tickets for the Olympics, but because of me, my mother missed the opening ceremony.

The house I grew up in is on the outskirts of Berlin but still within the city limits. The place is called Weinmeisterhöhe in the district of Spandau, about ten miles due west from the heart of the city. Spandau is where Berlin's two rivers, the Spree and the Havel, intersect. We were west of the Havel, where relatively few people lived, and (unlike most of Berlin, which is flat) the area was elevated. My father built the house on about a half hectare (or one acre) of land with a great view of the Havel River that formed into a lake directly below; the river was almost a kilometer, or about six-tenths of a mile, across.

I should say that my life, at least at the beginning, was a privileged one. Our house had several bedrooms, and even a separate wing for my paternal grandmother. We also had a live-in nanny and a cook.

Fräulein Grete, the nanny, I remember, was fairly young. We also had a tailor, an older woman, who would come and stay for several weeks each year. She did all of the sewing for the family, making new clothes. It was fairly unusual, but, in those days, my father's job earned him a good income, and so we were able to have such extras.

My family's house in Berlin.

My father was an aircraft design engineer who worked for the Junkers Aircraft Company. He had joined Junkers in the 1920s, and later became one of the head engineers after Junkers merged with Lufthansa, the German airline.

My father's life history is as twisted as the times in which he lived. He was born Werner Müller in 1894 in Duisburg, a town in Westphalia, but the family later moved to Kauffung in Silesia, which is now Polish. His father, my grandfather, was an industrialist involved in steel (or coal) production. He committed suicide during the 1920s. I heard two stories about the reason why: one said that he was desperate when his business failed during a financial crisis; the other that he did it when his affair with a household maid was discovered. I don't know which is true.

My father became a cadet at the German Naval Academy before World War I. During his naval training, he sailed to Central America, Cuba, and Florida. When World War I broke out in 1914, he was assigned to a cruiser and participated in several naval battles, including the biggest naval battle in World War I, the battle of Jutland, which took place in the Skagerrak Sound between Norway and Denmark. He wouldn't talk much about his war experiences in either world war, but I remember him talking about Jutland. He said that they could hardly see the opposing British vessels when they bombarded each other. "Sometimes you could only see the smoke from the chimneys above the horizon." It made the battle and the killings rather "impersonal." My father finished the war as a lieutenant.

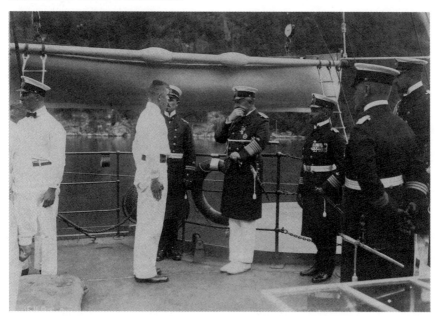

Kaiser Wilhelm II inspecting my father's ship, the SMS *Hertha*, c. 1913.

When World War I was over, under the Versailles Treaty ending the war, Germany could have no air force, no army, no navy; the country was limited to something equivalent to a national guard.

But those who had been in the former military thought, "Why did we lose this war? We were doing pretty well." In retrospect, we now know that the Nazis realized and exploited the fact that many ordinary Germans hadn't really believed that they had been defeated; they thought that there was some conspiracy of the Communists and the Jews against the German people. That was most likely at least partly due to the fact that World War I was mostly fought outside of Germany's borders.

The German people had been living under a monarchy with totalitarian tendencies; they heard nothing but positive propaganda. Then, all of a sudden, they read in the newspapers that the war was over and their country had lost. It was a non sequitur, leading to a nationwide case of cognitive dissonance.

When my father came back with thousands of other officers after World War I, he and the rest of them didn't know what to do. For the first time in his life, he became politically engaged. There were a lot of so-called "free corps," or former troops, banding together on their own. In Silesia, where my father had grown up, the Poles had taken over; so the former German troops started a private war in Silesia and drove the Poles out of the region. My father took part in that but, subsequent to that, he studied metallurgy at a university and received an engineering degree.

One of the other provisions of the Treaty of Versailles was to restrict Germany's ability to manufacture airplanes and fly them to other countries. To circumvent this, Junkers would build planes and then fly them to Sweden, which was a neutral country, where all the planes would get Swedish insignia. Afterward, they would fly them back to Germany and use them for civilian air travel within Germany—and to other countries.

It was during this same period, the mid-20s, when my father met my mother, who was also working at Junkers Aircraft. Her position was more or less that of a secretary because women were not encouraged to get advanced degrees—or high-level jobs—in those days.

My mother sometimes accompanied my father on his trips to Sweden. She told me that they once made an emergency landing in a field. Engine failure was not that rare at the time, and it was also not a big deal. The planes simply landed at the next suitable cornfield or other location. So for my parents the trip was like a boondoggle—fly to Sweden, get a nice meal, get the plane repainted, and fly back. The planes, of course, were commercial and passenger planes, not military. (Germany didn't start to redevelop its military until Hitler came to power in 1933.)

Both my parents were ardent skiers and they got engaged on New Year's Eve of '26 after they each had won prizes for second place in a ski race. They were living in Dessau at the time. (Not far from Berlin, Dessau is a town that is known mainly as the place where Walter Gropius founded the Bauhaus style—with its merging of architecture, art, and design.)

My parents were married in 1928. My mother had grown up in Hagen, in Westphalia, in a large family. Her father owned a company called Heyda Werke, which made paper products such as notebooks, diaries, office supplies, accounting ledgers, etc. She had one brother and three sisters. Early on, she helped in the family business and throughout her life was a very smart businesswoman. However, she left school after the tenth grade—as was considered appropriate for women—to attend a women's school that taught home economics and secretarial skills. From there, she got her job in Dessau, though I'm not exactly sure how.

My parents on the day of their engagement, New Year's Eve, 1926.

I believe that my parents must have moved to Berlin soon after their wedding. The move was probably connected to the merger of Junkers Aircraft and Deutsche Aero-Lloyd AG to form Luft Hansa (later "Lufthansa") Airlines. Lufthansa from the beginning had big ambitions to fly to Asia and to the Americas, while Junkers continued to design and manufacture planes. My father had to go to foreign countries to help sell planes. At one point, he went to Brazil to try to sell the Junkers Ju52 for flights inside South America. He flew on the *Graf Zeppelin* airship (a sister vessel to the *Hindenburg*) to Rio de Janeiro, a crossing that took something like ten days.

By that time, after years of political upheaval and economic hardship, Hitler had taken power in Germany. The *Graf Zeppelin* voyage was a big deal for the new Nazi regime, and they reported on its progress every day on the evening news. My mother followed this with a keen interest, nervous about my father's transatlantic flight. One day, when the zeppelin was over southern France, there was no report on the radio. My mother called the radio station in a panic, and they told her that because of heavy headwinds the zeppelin had actually lost ground that day—and the Nazis didn't allow that information to be broadcast.

Graf Zeppelin arriving in Rio de Janeiro, November 1935.

The arrival of the *Graf Zeppelin* caused a sensation in Rio de Janeiro. Next came the main event. The Junkers Ju52 was to compete in a race against the American DC-3, with both planes flying from Rio to Santiago de Chile. The Junkers plane went first and made it—barely—across the Andes Mountains as clouds billowed up in a gathering storm. The DC-3 left thirty minutes later; it could actually climb higher than the Ju52, but by that time the clouds were forming at altitudes too high even for it, and it had to turn back. The Ju52 was chosen by the local airline, and my father returned triumphant on an ocean liner, the *Cap Arcona*. He had been one of the main designers of the Ju52 and was responsible for it having three engines for safety reasons rather than one or two engines that were then common. My father never flew planes himself—he had very little manual dexterity (couldn't even hit a nail on the head!)—and was what you call a theoretical engineer. But he was apparently very good at what he did.

My brother, Jürgen, was born in 1929; my sister, Gisela, in 1932. As I already mentioned, I was born in the summer of 1936, just a few days before the start of what became known as the Jesse Owens Olympics. (Defying Nazi claims of Aryan superiority, the African-American sprinter famously won four gold medals in front of the Führer, a total racist, who by many accounts refused to shake the black man's hand—something Owens himself later refuted.) My parents called me the "Olympic Baby."

1936 Berlin Summer Olympics, scoreboard; photo taken by my father.

TWO

WAR

My earliest memory is of the day World War II began. It was the first of September, 1939—the day Germany invaded Poland.

I had just turned three. According to common belief, that is normally too young to remember anything, but when something historic like this happens, and you have a memory of it, you can later in life figure out what it must have been.

When I went downstairs for breakfast that morning, I heard my mother crying in the kitchen. The nanny and the cleaning lady were there, and they were all crying. So I stopped and asked, "Why are you crying?" My mother said, "Something terrible has just happened. There is another war." I didn't really know what that meant, but when I heard the words "something terrible" and "war" I remember sitting down and not even going into the kitchen, just sitting down on the bottom step of the stairway and crying. I have a vivid memory of that. I don't remember anything else happening, however. Life seemed to simply go on as before.

But Father was drafted right away. He was forty-six years old. I have no memory of him leaving or saying goodbye. But I remember being aware that he was gone.

Father had been in the navy in World War I, but in World War II he was drafted into the air force as a captain because of his knowledge of planes. He was stationed all over the place, mostly outside of Germany. After all, early on, the war did not take place within Germany's borders. This was the expansionary phase. My father found himself in Poland, in the Balkan campaign, and traveling all the way down to Crete, in the regiment of Richthofen, the son of the Red Baron. At that time, they were using the Junkers commercial planes as transport planes, particularly for dropping parachutists. He was also in Bulgaria, Romania, Greece, and probably Hungary

His role was to be at an air force base where the planes took off and came back, to supervise repair jobs on the planes—including bombers—which had been damaged, and to make sure that they were in proper operating condition.

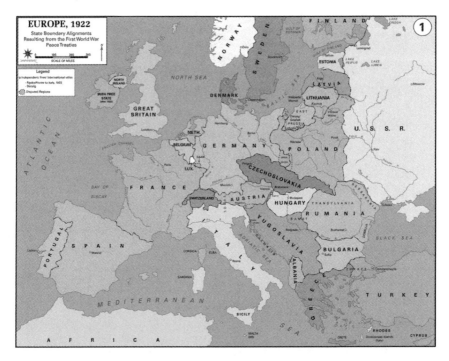

Later in the war, my father was promoted to major. He came home for the holidays or on leave three or four times a year, and we were delighted. He would be in uniform, and arrive with a driver in a military vehicle, like a jeep, and the driver would let me play with the instruments. Sometimes my father would stay for three or four days, sometimes as long as a week. But he could never talk about what he had been doing during the war. The same was true when we got mail from him. It was "military mail." It didn't say where he was. He couldn't say, "Today, I'm in Hungary at such-and-such air force base." It was all classified.

Our household stayed in place—for a while—after the war began. But, slowly, the staff dissolved: our nanny went away once I started school; our cook also went away, leaving us on our own except for the couple occupying another—smaller—house on our property that my parents owned. The couple that lived there would help us out, though I am not certain why the husband was not in the war.

With my father, 1940.

My brother, Jürgen, who was seven years older than I, had to join the Hitler Youth, which was sort of like the Boy Scouts (the Soviet Union had a similar organization called the "Young Pioneers"). And my sister, Gisela, the middle child in our family, had to join the *Bund Deutscher Mädel* (*BDM*), which was the League of German Girls—the female equivalent of the Hitler Youth. They were automatically signed up in school, and were taken on hiking trips. And, at first, Jürgen and Gisela had fun being in the groups.

My sister and brother had a far deeper understanding of what was occurring during the war years than did I, because I was so young. When I recently discussed those years with my sister, I asked her what she had known about Hitler as a schoolgirl.

She said she understood that Hitler was the leader, our Führer, and that she and her classmates had to salute him regularly.

At camp, we had to do a flag parade every morning and then raise our arms . . . well, you know . . . SA [short for Sturmabteilung, the original paramilitary wing of the Nazi Party] marching. The whole school had to sing the two flag songs every morning. That was an order. Everybody had to do the same . . . . We never spoke about Hitler, though. We all had to become Jungmädels [join the Young Girls League]. That was girls under fourteen or so. We wore a Tracht *[traditional costume], or a* Kluft *as it was called at the time. That was something special of course. You got a neckerchief. The skirt was buttoned onto the white blouse, no waistband. It was simply buttoned on. And somehow you were proud of that.*

They gave us an extra afternoon of voluntary sports every week. I loved doing sports, so that was great for me. The Hitler Youth organized what was called Heimabende, *or "domestic evenings." And Mother didn't want me to take part in those kinds of activities, so she always scheduled my piano lessons for the same time. Once a week there would be a sports day and* Heimabend. *I won the Siegernadel, the Hitler Youth sports pin, at the Olympic Stadium and I came home all happy. But I didn't get my Siegernadel. Because you had to take part in* Heimabend *in order to get your Siegernadel. The pressure was there. I scolded Mother. "How can you let this happen?" I wanted my Siegernadel like everybody else.*

Gisela also told me about an incident from early in my life—one of which I have no recollection—that illustrates just how pervasive Nazi influence was in everyday German life from the time the Nazis assumed power in the early 1930s.

Grandmother saw to it that you could describe the pictures in books at a very early age, and you would memorize the text. And then you would say, "Let me read you a book." You would point to the pictures and recite the text by heart. I still remember one of the poems. There's an illustration of a little boy and a fat farm pig. And beneath the picture it says: "Jochen comes home after playing. Oh boy, just look at him! What does Jochen look like? Even the pig is perplexed and shudders and says, 'Yuck, Jochen, are you dirty! Not even I am that dirty."

Then the NSDAP [Nazi Party] came—they interfered in families' lives right from the start. They had, so-to-speak, "discovered" you and decided that you should recite a poem on the radio for Mother's Day. There was a small cafe or restaurant on the Weinmeisterhöhe, nothing to write home about, but it worked as a gathering room. And one day they put you on a tall chair in the cafe and you recited your Mother's Day poem.

"When early the dear sun awakes,
my heart sings and whistles and laughs.
So wonderful the world,

so wonderful to be at home with our sweet mother dear.
My heart is happy and that is so."

And you recited it so well that there was not a dry eye in the house. And
you got a lot of laughter and applause.

According to Gisela, our mother had actually not wanted to take part in this
event organized by the Nazis and that, in her own quiet, mostly very careful
manner, she had resisted the Nazis in other ways over the years. For example,
there was one unpleasant exchange involving Mother and a local Nazi leader
after Father had gone off to war.

The Nazi leader in our neighborhood was the mother of a friend of mine,
a Mrs. Weber. And this Mrs. Weber, she would go out of her mind at
the mere mention of the name Hitler. She was totally nuts. And she told
Mother, "You are the only one on the entire Weinmeisterhöhe who doesn't
darn socks for the soldiers! You could also darn some socks for the soldiers."
And Mother replied, "I have three children whom I have to raise on my
own. I have the big house and a garden. I have enough to do. I don't think
Hitler would expect me to also darn socks for the soldiers." And she left.

The two women became very hostile toward each other.

During those years the government had what they called the *Winterhilfswerk*,
or "Winter Relief." It was a charity campaign organized by the Nazis—but you
didn't necessarily know that. The civilian volunteers went around with wooden
carts, up and down the streets, stopping at every house. You were required to
contribute stuff that you didn't need any more—clothes, money, whatever. You
couldn't just say, "Sorry, but I am not participating in this."

On Hitler's birthday, the twentieth of April, you had to hang the Nazi flag out of some window. If you didn't, you would have "a visit" the next day. All of this, the people just did to avoid any trouble.

With everything that was around me, when I was very young, I was already aware that Hitler was our leader—that he was the big man.

My sister, Gisela, and me (far right), wearing a Nazi helmet.

We, of course, would listen to the Führer on the radio. Radio broadcasts were a very formal affair in those days. You sat down and listened. The broadcast wasn't simply some sort of background noise; it was the center of activity. There were a few things we listened to. Obviously, if Hitler made a speech—his speeches would be broadcast at a certain time—we would tune in. The second thing we listened to was any breaking news from the front. In the early years of the war, everything that came out of the radio was a fancy announcement of another victory—breaking news you might say. It would be preceded by, I think it was a few notes of Beethoven's Fifth—*Da-da-da, duh. Da-da-da, da-da*—and then came the announcer's voice: "*This is a special announcement from the Führer's headquarters.*" The next thing would be another voice from *Das Hauptkommando der Wehrmacht,* or the chief command center of the Wehrmacht, announcing: "*Germans have captured Warsaw,*" or something like that. The announcement was usually pretty brief, and then the music would resume, and it was over. This happened once or twice a week.

We also listened to classical music, which my mother liked. Listening to the radio was always really magical, because we would often sit in the dark, or with just a small lamp lit. My mother would turn on the radio. At first, there would be no sound, but slowly the dim white light on the face of the radio would turn a bright green as the tubes warmed up.

We also sat in the dark because of the possibility of air raids. Sitting in the dark wasn't a big deal because we had been taught never to leave a light on that wasn't actually needed. It was about saving money. Electricity was very expensive in Germany. Everybody did it, and many still do. It's just the thrifty nature of people.

Though we spent many evenings in the dark, my memories get much more vivid by 1941, when I was four or five, when the Allied air raids of Germany began.

The Germans had repeatedly bombed London during the *Blitzkrieg* in 1940–41. Hitler said then that Germany was concentrating its attacks on railroad stations and industrial targets, or factories and things like that. And—as far as I know—it started off that way on both sides, but there was collateral damage in the form of civilian casualties from the beginning.

By 1941, after the London blitz, it was as if the Allies were sending us the message, "Now we're coming your way."

The local authorities installed sirens on many rooftops. While we didn't have one on our roof, the other sirens were close enough so that we could always hear them well. To me, the sirens were fascinating because there were various types of siren sounds. There was the *Voralarm,* or pre-alarm, in which sirens blared in intervals with short pauses in between, indicating that enemy aircraft were approaching and it was time to seek shelter. Then came the *Vollalarm*, in which the sounds of the sirens came in continuous short bursts, warning that attack was imminent. And finally we had the *Entwarnung*, the "all-safe" signal, a continuous siren emission lasting for about a minute to let us know that the threat had passed.

We didn't have a bunker, in the beginning. When we had the first air raid, we went into our basement and that was very, very scary—probably the scariest time for me as a kid that I can remember. I was about five. The basement room was essentially a large pantry, perhaps ten by twenty feet in size; it had jars and jars of preserves made from fruit from the fruit trees on our property, as well as vegetables that we would eat in the winter. My mother, my brother and sister, and my Grandmother and I sat in that room, in the dark with all the lights turned off. I know everybody must have been pretty pale. There was no screaming. No crying. Everybody was very quiet. I think we sat there for about an hour.

The second time, however, it was already less frightening because I had survived the first time. Initially, the air raids only occurred in the middle of the night. My mother would wake us up and we would troop down to the basement. Whenever there was actually some activity—when some bombs would fall in the area—all the glass jars would rattle and some would actually fall off the shelves right behind us. The first time it happened I immediately thought we had just gotten hit by a bomb.

My sister's recollections of those events are very similar to mine. She was nine at the time.

When they started bombing Germany, very early on we assumed that Berlin would also get hit. And I remember sitting with Grandmother in the cellar with wet cloths that we could quickly put on our faces if we were to get hit; we would sit in reclining lawn chairs, so it was a bit like being in bed. The cellar was very primitive. It wasn't protected at all; it wasn't a bomb shelter. We'd sit down there in between the jars of jam and the heaps of coal with those cloths. We thought right away that there would be gas bombs. There was always this talk of gas, and how you wouldn't be able to breathe it in for long before you'd suffocate. That's what I was afraid of. That's what I was really afraid of. But there was no gas. None at all.

Grandmother would always sit next to me. And once, when a bomb zoomed past our house, with a loud whistling sound, Grandmother took my hand and said, "My dear, we need to say good-bye." She was convinced that our house had been directly hit. Now that scared the living daylights out of me! But children forget quickly and we were glad that we had survived. And I wasn't really conscious of the potential horror because I had never experienced an exploding bomb. We didn't really know how that would manifest itself. I think we were still too young.

As the bombing intensified, it became clear that it wasn't safe to be in the house—even in the basement—and my father organized the construction of an underground bunker in the front yard, about twenty yards from the house. He hired men who dug a big hole, in which they laid huge cement pipes that served as the bunker. There were benches inside, and you could sit across from one another without touching. The interior was maybe six feet by six or seven feet, and perhaps ten feet long, with a ventilation shaft. The entrance door lay level to the ground and could be lifted up by two handles; beneath the door were the stairs leading down to the bunker, and another door at the bottom of the stairs to access the tubular sitting area. On top of the bunker was a huge pile of sand. The bunker held up through the war, and is still there today. In fact, decades later, I took my own children and grandchildren to see it.

By 1943, when I turned seven, I no longer really heard the sirens. They had become almost like background noise, like the sound of a nearby subway. We were in the bunker at least four times a week. My mother would wake me up and say it was time to go down to the bunker. I would stumble down, go outside, go to the bunker, lie down, and go right back to sleep.

Where we were—in what amounted to the suburbs—it was fairly common for families to have their own bunkers because there weren't communal air raid shelters. In the city center, everybody had to go to air raid shelters that the government had built of massively thick concrete. They were pretty safe, even though they were mostly above ground, because Berlin has a very high underground water level.

The thing about the bombing that made it hard to plan for was that there were all kinds of bombs being used. Most bombs were not really filled with heavy explosives. A lot of them were incendiary bombs that just caused fires, but didn't do a lot of damage otherwise. Of course, there were detonating bombs as well. If we would have had a direct hit from one of those—thankfully the possibility was low—it would have killed us. In addition, there was a third type we called an "air mine." It was a bomb that detonated when it hit the ground and spread shrapnel horizontally, over hundreds of meters. Air mine bombs scared us the most.

With my grandchildren, visiting my family's WWII bunker built by my father, 2011.

Bunker entrance.

We always knew when we had bomb activity right in our area because the noise would get louder and other sounds could be heard. We knew that when the planes came in at night they would fly over us headed to downtown Berlin. Of course you couldn't see them, you could only hear them, but then we would see the nearby searchlights of a German artillery (*Flak*) station that was less than a half-mile from our house. The searchlights would scan the sky for planes to shoot down. Sometimes, we would even stand outside and watch. Though it changed as the war progressed, at first there was very little chance that the Allies would randomly release bombs, because they had specific missions, district by district—and the suburbs weren't high priority targets.

The British—it was more the British than the Americans—didn't care much about a suburb such as ours, but they attacked the nearby flak station and inflicted collateral damage on our house and on others in the neighborhood. That's why Weinmeisterhöhe lost a number of houses. (They did eventually knock out the station, but that was later, when we were already out of Berlin.)

After bombs hit in our area, it was great fun for us kids to go out the next morning with tin cans and collect the debris. We tried to identify the fragments of heavy metal. Some were still hot and some had threads. Even as young children, we were aware of the different types of bombs, and we quickly learned which pieces belonged to which kind of explosive device. We thought it was better than stamp collecting because it was really exciting. My friends and I would trade pieces. The "best" pieces of shrapnel to find were ones with a serial number, because then the shrapnel was distinguishable. And the second best were really large, two- or three-inch pieces of jagged metal that had been blown apart and looked like thorns. When we found those, we were pretty happy, even though it wasn't all that hard to find them because the terrain was very flat and you could spot them from a distance.

Although it sounds like a horrible life when you read about it, I wasn't particularly traumatized by any of this. You have to realize that children very quickly get used to almost anything. It was harder on my older siblings because they were already in school when the war broke out and they were more afraid because they understood the gravity of the situation. But, for us younger kids, it was just a big game.

I remember the first time our house was directly hit by a bomb; it was in '42 or '43. We were in the bunker, and my brother and the man who lived in the other house on our property would occasionally peer outside to make sure our house was okay. Only, this time, my brother signaled that the house had been hit and that there was a fire. Although we hadn't yet heard the all-clear siren, we ran in to extinguish the fire with sand and water—buckets of which my mother kept in each room for that exact purpose. (If we had waited until the air raid was over, the whole house would have burned down.)

The incendiary devices, depending on the angle at which they hit a house, either went all the way through and into the basement or got stuck in the attic, or somewhere in between. Once they started bombing our area of town, we usually saw some kind of fire when we emerged, and we would all race into the house. It was risky. There was always a possibility that there might be another bomb dropped while we were dousing the fire if they had not yet given the all-clear signal. You had to take a chance if you wanted to save the house.

One time, an incendiary device came through the roof and landed in my grandmother's bed. (Of course she was in the bunker.) The adults in the bunker rushed up into the house, and they threw the whole bed out the window. Fortunately, only the bed was burning.

Preparing as you left the house was important. Even if you didn't sustain a direct hit, the air mines could blast out all your windows because of the pressure. So, before going into the bunker, we would open all the windows, even in the middle of the winter. In 1942–43, the roof of our house was—or rather the tiles on the roof were—blown off five times because of the air pressure from bombs exploding nearby. We had the windows protected, but the roof was covered with ceramic tiles, which could only withstand so much. Four times, my father managed to have them replaced, which was very difficult during the war, but he was a good organizer. Finally, after the fifth time, the workers nailed sheet metal on the roof—and that's how the house survived the war.

The Allies would also drop "Christmas trees"—or at least that's what we called them. They were like huge, illuminated flares, almost like fireworks. For a moment or two, they would illuminate the whole countryside below us as they slowly descended. Their purpose was to make it easier for the bombers to find their targets, but the displays they made were beautiful, mostly white lights.

Really, everything for children becomes normal—as long as you survive.

There is one story that does stand out from that time; it illustrates both my naiveté and the fact that even in the midst of the war, life went on.

Jürgen was in the living room with his girlfriend, and he wanted me to get lost—so he made up a story. He said, "You know what? Hitler is going to be appearing at the movie theater in Gatow" (the next town over).

With my mother and siblings, Berlin, 1942.

By then, I was old enough to realize that to see Hitler in person would have been pretty interesting. Keep in mind, there was no television, and I never went to the movie houses where they showed the newsreels in which Hitler paraded around. I had only seen photographs of him.

So, thinking it would be a big deal to get to see the Führer, I was excited, I set out on my own to Gatow. I knew exactly where that was because it wasn't far from my school. It was about a three-mile hike, and the shoes I was wearing were really painful and gave me blisters. When I got there, there was nothing. And so I came home, mad as hell. I think it was an April Fool's Day joke because I remember my brother and his girlfriend saying "April Fool!"

In the fall of 1942, at age six, I started elementary school; there was no kindergarten. The elementary school was pretty far from our house. We were in a little residential area, so my friends and I had to take a bus—a public bus, since there were no school buses—to the school. We walked ten minutes to the stop. We did all of this on our own, even at just six years old. There was no babysitter accompanying us. The society was not as overprotective as our society is today. Of course there was very little crime in the suburbs. I would be sent off with my lunch: a sandwich with black bread and maybe an apple or a pear—no bananas; we didn't have bananas. (I never saw a banana until I was fourteen years old.)

A WWII-era one-man roadside air raid shelter in Germany.

Partway through the school year, the buses began to show up with pieces of cardboard in the windows rather than glass, because they had been damaged from bombing the night before. Eventually, the buses stopped coming, but it happened incrementally. At first, they came less regularly, and we would begin to walk to school, which was about three miles. I remember we would constantly look back just to see if a bus was coming, and if we saw a bus, we would run as fast as we could to the next stop. But we couldn't rely on the buses, and at times we had to walk the entire way.

Later on, there would sometimes be air raids during the day, on our way home from school. German air defenses had pretty much collapsed by then. When the sirens went off and if it was a nice day, we could see the armada of planes going overhead and hear a deep humming sound made by their propeller engines. They looked like little silver fish in the sky. We knew that there was no immediate danger, because they were going to the city itself. But when they came back, they sometimes randomly released bombs that were left in the bomb bays of the planes to lighten their loads for the return flights. It was then that we would go into one of the one-man air raid shelters that were sitting at intervals along the street. Several of us could squeeze into one of them, and we were scared.

The government, meanwhile, had decided to evacuate the children from Berlin. My brother's school, the Kant Gymnasium, was sent—teachers and students—to the countryside, several hundred miles east, to a place called Litzmannstadt, which is now in Poland. And my sister's school was moved by train to a place in Saxony, near Leipzig. Then there was the question as to what to do with me, since I was too young to be evacuated without my parents.

At one point, my mother took me to Leipzig to live with her sister, my aunt, because Leipzig was considered safer than Berlin—and my aunt's husband was a U-boat captain, so he wasn't around. My mother made me go to school there, which was the first time that I was really, truly miserable. It had nothing to do with the war. It had to do with the way I was treated by the local kids. Leipzig is in Saxony, and my classmates hated Berlin and Berliners—in part because we had a different accent. I had always been a popular boy, but in that school I was tormented—not just by the kids, but by the teachers, too. The kids would taunt me and throw stones, so I had to be picked up from school every day. It became so bad that the experiment only lasted for a couple of weeks before my mother and I returned to Berlin.

Back home, I showed up at our elementary school one day only to discover that it had burned down; it had taken a direct hit. Of course, we kids were delighted. You know, as strange as it may sound, that was probably one of the very few days that I missed school during the entire war. The next day, the school was back in session, relocated to a building owned by a landscaping business. The administrators just moved everybody into the space, even though it was crowded—and a lot of school supplies had been destroyed.

By the time I was six or seven, I had already started reading the newspaper that my parents subscribed to, every day. The papers had all been "Nazified," but they kept their old names. Before the war the *Deutsche Allgemeine Zeitung* (*"German General Newspaper"*) had been a sort of a democratic, centrist, reasonable paper. After the Nazis took it over, its headlines became more sensational and partisan. However, what the paper did have were maps showing where the front lines were, and I remember poring over those maps. In those days, most of the action was in Russia, and I was following that, convinced, of course, that Germany would win the war.

It never occurred to me that the outcome might be otherwise. The paper was so suffused with propaganda, winning was a given. Whenever there was a setback, the reports never said that the German troops retreated. Instead, they would say that the German troops went into prepared positions. Only those positions happened to be behind the previous positions. Even as a young child I got wind of that fairly quickly.

However, there were other things I didn't know as much about back then. The horrible mistreatment of Jews, for instance. Or the concentration camps.

My sister, three years older than I, has told me that nobody spoke about any of this at home. Maybe our parents and Grandmother spoke about them, she said, but only after we went to bed. As for politics, she told me she couldn't remember that we, as children, engaged with the politics of our country in any way (aside from being members of the youth groups—which we weren't aware were political).

There were also no SA men in our vicinity. And we didn't initially know about any Jews being picked up because we had no contact with Jews. Others had noticed that there were people missing, but we didn't have missing people in our neighborhood. Early on in the war, we really did grow up just like before.

But there was at least one incident that Gisela participated in that haunts her to this day, more than seven decades later.

Around the corner there was a pretty, tall brick building that I always called the haunted house. Mother would go—this was already during the war—around with a donation list for the Winter Relief program. And sometimes I would accompany her. We would always stop at this house, which belonged to the Lorands, a Jewish family. She was an actress and he had been an actor. And she always made a donation. Mother would exchange a few friendly words with her.

My girlfriends told me that Hitler's men had picked her husband up. "They hanged him! He was hanging there with his tongue sticking out!" We kids would go to her street—I was five at the time—and when Mrs. Lorand appeared, we would all stick out our tongues at her. That's how kids are. When I think about that today, I have a very, very bad conscience, because she was really a lovely lady.

After the war I said to Mother, "They say there were large transports from Berlin train stations." She said, "Well, they told us that they were being taken to safety. That they were being taken to camps that were appropriate for them. That's all we heard!"

The German media, of course, made no mention of the camps either, though they did regularly publish unflattering depictions of Jews, blaming them for this or that, all part of the national hysteria that the Nazis whipped up.

I didn't know too much about casualties either. My first cousin, the son of my father's sister (who was many years older than I), had been killed during the Poland campaign very early in the war—in the very first week. Another cousin, the very young son of one of my mother's sisters, was also killed soon after being sent to war, as was his father. Both mothers died childless, though I never knew either of the boys or my uncle.

In the first years of the war, even as a young boy, I could see the infrastructure starting to crumble, the roads and the bridges. And there were shortages of many of the things you take for granted, such as fuel, food, and toilet paper. We would cut up the daily newspaper, and use it as toilet paper.

Rationing started shortly after the beginning of the war, perhaps in 1940. We each would get an allotment of so many grams of fat and so many grams of this and that, all of which would be indicated on a monthly ration card. The card was divided into three ten-day periods to prevent you from using your whole month's supplies at once. The ration office didn't want you to starve to death, so you could only use the first set of coupons for the first ten days, and then you had to wait for the next ten days, and then for the ten days after that. You would receive your card and go to the grocery store. For example, you would ask the clerk for fifty grams of butter (just short of two ounces), and she would clip out the coupon with scissors, and give you the butter—she would only give it to you if you had the coupon, but you still had to pay for it.

There was a pecking order; they had various kinds of cards. If you did hard physical work, however, the ration office would increase your allotment. The standard amount of supplies for our family in a single period would barely have been enough for one person during better times. But my ration was enough for me. I had never been a big eater, so I never felt any scarcity or hunger or anything until after the war. My mother never resented the rationing. For her, it was nothing compared to World War I; people really starved during *that* war.

As the rationing went on, the air raids continued. At night, we could see the whole city in flames from our suburban hill. I mean—various parts of the city each night. Berlin was too large for the whole city to be bombed at once. Sometimes it was down here, sometimes it was over there; the Allies were taking one district at a time—"carpet-bombing." Everything went up in flames. Finally, one night, my mother said, "We have to get out." Father agreed. He said, "You have to move. We can't keep you here in Berlin."

In reality, it was pretty dangerous. The war was accelerating very quickly. My mother became very nervous and stressed because she was running the household, dealing with the rations, and almost every night at the first sound of the sirens, making sure we were in the bunker. Then, one day, my father came home and said, "It's all organized. Tomorrow we are going east to Bottschow."

Bottschow is a village on the other side of the Oder River (east of Berlin). My father knew the area wasn't a target—in fact, during the entire war it did not experience a single air raid. The place, only ninety kilometers (almost sixty miles) from Berlin, is now in Poland; it's called Boczów.

Not understanding what was at stake, I said, "No, I don't want to leave. All my friends are here. My school is here." Father gave me a big speech about how beautiful the place was; he said that the house we were going to was "a castle and has a cupola, and everything." I said, "Well, is there a king in this castle?" I thought a castle had to have a king. He said, "No, there's no king, but it is a real castle." So he won me over. I ran across the street to tell my best buddy, Peter Babikow. When I told him that we were leaving he was pretty sad. But I didn't care. I was too excited.

We had survived Berlin—for now.

THREE

ON THE ROAD

My father immediately had to go back to the front, so it was just my mother, my grandmother and I—and our driver—in the car going to Bottschow the next day (my siblings were still away at their schools). Because we lived on the western edge of the city, in order to go east, we had to traverse all of Berlin. For the first time in my life, I saw real devastation. It was mid–1943. I was seven years old.

As we drove through the streets, we saw areas where virtually every building had been set ablaze—flames shot up, but there were no firefighters, no nothing. People were moving around like ghosts, trying to salvage things here and there. I couldn't believe the destruction. The streets had been sort of cleared, so that a car could pass through, but just barely. It was extremely quiet, except for the crackling of the flames. That's what I remember.

My mother kept repeating, "This is horrible; this is horrible. This is horrible." She was really depressed, which for her was unusual. She generally had an upbeat attitude. I didn't see any corpses lying around in the street, but I knew then that—*wow*—a lot of people had been killed. I finally knew why we were leaving Berlin. That's when I became really frightened—a feeling that was very unexpected.

My mother had told me that we were at war with England, France, America, and Russia, and that they were sending over bombers to bomb us. But my understanding had been very limited. For me, there had *always* been war. That was the normal state of affairs. It had never occurred to me that, most of the time, there is no war. At that point, I was old enough to question why they were dropping bombs on us, why they were doing any of it. It finally dawned on me that life was pretty unusual.

Of course, in the classroom we didn't hear anything about the war. We were taught only the traditional subjects: reading, writing, and the like. I found out later that the same was true for Jürgen and Gisela. They were reading the classics, and there was never any discussion about the war.

Bombed-out Berlin.

I had a hard time wrapping my head around it all. Even though the Brits were doing a lot of the bombing, everybody seemed to hate the Russians. It had to do with the German attitude about people, the sense that Germanic people were superior to Slavic people. Hitler had actually been an admirer of

Britain. But Britain had made an agreement that if Poland were invaded, it would declare war—and they did. That came as a shock to Hitler. His bluff had been called. He considered the English and most Americans as equal to the Germans—Aryan people—and tried to avoid having to go to war with them. Ironically enough, he was the one who declared war on America. (That was one of the most insane things he did. He had no clue as to what America was all about.)

The "castle" in Bottschow that my father had promised me turned out to be a big country house, but it seemed like a castle. It belonged to a family called "von Bonin" whom my parents knew. The area was almost feudalistic; it was in old East Prussia. Basically, Mr. von Bonin was the big landowner in town. I think everybody in the town, or "village" rather, was dependent on him.

When we arrived, we were assigned rooms. I remember mine was on one of the top floors, pretty high up, and I was very excited. (Change has always excited me.) Mr. von Bonin was away in the war—he was an officer. In the house was just his wife—a young, pretty woman who was in charge and very friendly. I think there may have been some other people living there as well, but I don't remember them. Of course, it was such a big house that it would have been easy not to run into another person.

There was a separate house for the staff and some of the laborers, who worked the fields; some of them lived there. There was a full-time cook, who provided meals for both the workers and the family from the enormous kitchen. At the dinner table there would be perhaps ten people, and, because it was a farming area, there always seemed to be enough food.

Both of my grandmothers occasionally came for long stays; I think my *grosse* grandmother—my Berlin grandmother—may have actually been with us most of the time since she had accompanied my mother and me from Berlin. (I never knew my grandfathers; both of whom had died before I was born.) Jürgen and Gisela also joined us, once we were settled in the countryside.

The three of us had to go to school. I went to the local school, which was a one-room schoolhouse with children from first through eighth grade—nobody from the village went beyond eighth grade. We were all there in the one room, with one teacher. My sister and brother, however, had to take a half-hour ride on a local train every day to Frankfurt an der Oder (the Frankfurt in the east), which had the nearest high school.

Living in Bottschow provided us with a great sense of normalcy—even a certain monotony. It was a small village with a population of some two hundred people. There was nothing there. It was bucolic, very peaceful. There were no air raids, and my mother was able to relax. We all relaxed.

For me, the place was fun. My brother and I would go up to the attic, which was enormous, and set up a model train set so that the train would disappear behind walls and chimneys, and then come back. I found it exciting. Outside were fields and woods as well as a lake, where we could swim—all of which was very private.

Everyone was nice and friendly. People were only bothered by normal daily aggravations. Our school routine was occasionally interrupted when potato weevils infested the fields. We would have to go out and search every single potato plant for the insects and, if we found them, collect them. We also had to help during the potato harvest. We were given baskets, and when our baskets were full, we would walk down the row in which we worked to a collection point; for each basket we would receive a few pennies compensation from the farmer.

Working in the fields was the first time I saw Russian prisoners of war. They worked right alongside us. They didn't wear special clothes or prison uniforms; they were dressed like everybody else. I wouldn't have known who they were, but somebody said that they were Russian POWs. They were quite friendly; some of them even spoke some German—broken German. It was also the first time that I met people whose first language wasn't German. I told my mother about them and how nice they were. She said, "Yes, because they're happy to be out of the war. You know, they have it much better here than they would if they were fighting for the Russians." And that's probably true. Of course, later on, when Stalin recaptured these people, many of them were sent to prison camps, or "reeducation" camps. Many were killed. But, for the time being, they worked— as far as I could tell—without any German soldiers, or anyone in uniform with weapons guarding them. They appeared healthy and well fed. I don't know where they stayed, but maybe they slept in nearby barracks.

They were twice as fast—not just twice as fast, ten times as fast as we were! Of course they were around twenty-five years old and we were only seven and eight. But it was amazing when you saw these guys gathering potatoes. Perhaps they had been peasants in Russia and used to it. Eventually, I found out that the prisoners weren't paid anything. I thought that was not really fair.

Sometime after moving to Bottschow, I remember sitting in the castle garden with my siblings and my mother—she liked to have afternoon tea outside whenever the day was nice. She looked at us and said, "You know, children, I have to tell you something. You cannot tell anybody, under any circumstances. Your father called and said the war is lost after the battle of Stalingrad." (The battle took place from August 23, 1942, to February 2, 1943.)

That came as a big shock to me, in spite of the fact that I had noticed that the German lines on the maps had fallen back. I could tell my mother knew more than she was letting on. But no one, not my brother nor my sister, spoke about it afterward. Stalingrad, for the Germans, was the turning point of the war. In reality, the war was already "unwinnable" when Hitler confronted Britain and America in the west, and the Soviet Union in the east. After World War I, the German military was of the opinion that the greatest mistake had been to fight on two fronts, and that that should never be repeated. Of course, Hitler, the "great strategist," ignored that advice.

In the summer of 1944, while we were still in Bottschow, we learned that there had been an assassination attempt on Hitler. We found out about it in the papers, and on the radio, but by the time we heard the news, it was already clear that Hitler had survived. Even so, there had been an initial belief among the conspirators that Hitler was dead because a bomb placed in a briefcase had detonated right next to his leg. And so they put a plan in place to take over the government in Berlin. When the news came that Hitler was alive, everything fell apart. A lot of people were arrested and executed. I was a little bit surprised that the attempt had happened, since clearly any opposition to Hitler had never been publicized before.

I had just turned eight years old, and, as I recall it, I personally was relieved and happy that Hitler didn't get killed; I felt glad that the Führer had survived the attempt. On a certain level, Hitler had always been presented as a father figure—like Stalin was presented to the Russian people—who would lead us to greater heights. I didn't learn until later that this was typical for any dictatorship. The dictator is always presented as an all-knowing, wise father to the people. In a democratic country, like the US or Britain, that would never fly.

During the time we were in Bottschow, as far as I know, my father was stationed in Italy, working at the Fiat factory in Turin, which had been converted to make airplanes. He gave me an Italian-made bicycle for my birthday. It was my first bicycle, and it was quite a thrill.

Prior to Italy, he had been maintaining the airplanes at different air force bases—in the Balkans and in the Ukraine.

Gisela recalled that he seemed to fly to "secluded" regions.

Father would tell us about all the places where he had made emergency landings, in the steppe, and here and there. He once said that he had been in the Crimea. He said, "The area is much too nice to stage war there. It's a beautiful spot. When we have peace again, we should go there for vacation."

And when he came back from Bulgaria, he would talk about how the people would pamper him, and tell us that the women were neat as a button. They would bake lovely breads and cakes and feed him. So in return he would buy things from them. And once, he brought me back an embroidered dress,

made entirely of rough linen. I don't think you ever saw it. It had a very
wide cross, made with a tiny cross-stitch. Absolutely beautiful, embroidered
in blue and red.

My father would come to visit us in Bottschow from time to time. His last visit
was in the middle of the winter—it would have been in early January of '45; the
Russians were knocking on Germany's door. For weeks and weeks and weeks,
from my bedroom window, while doing my homework, I had seen nothing but
German military equipment—trucks and tanks—headed west, moving away
from the Eastern Front. The Germans were in retreat, which confirmed what I
had already understood: the war was not going the way it was supposed to go.
We could hear the artillery fire, even from a considerable distance. We called it
Stalin's organ, because to us it sort of sounded like organ music.

When my father arrived, he said, "What? You're still here? I have to get
you out of here." Each village, each district had a Nazi commander, and those
local Nazi leaders had forbidden the population to flee—because it would show
a defeatist attitude. The people remaining in the villages were all women and
children who had been frozen in their tracks. This included my mother and our
hostess, Frau von Bonin.

My sister remembered another incident from that time that showed just
how desperate my father considered the situation to be for the Germans.

Everybody was already saying behind closed doors, "We can't win anymore."
And I thought, "Oh my God, oh my God, oh my God!" No one can imagine
how a war plays itself out, how it ends. We listened to the radio every eve-
ning, the position of the front lines.

After listening to one report, Father said . . . in front of me, "That's no
longer true. That's from two days ago. They [the Soviets] are already closer.
They're already over the German border. They're already in East Prussia."

*And Mother said, "Werner, you're going to get yourself into hot water."
And he almost fell on his face with . . . what was his name? . . . Hofmeier,
the one who was in charge of the farmstead in Bottschow, and was also the
local Nazi leader.*

*Another time he blurted out something about the Ukrainians. He said,
"They are good people. Clean and hard working. We should really be cre-
ating an alliance with them." And Mother said, "Can't you be more careful,
Werner?"*

*Father told Mrs. von Bonin, who was very pregnant, "Pack only the most
necessary things and go first to Berlin. You've got a place to stay there and
then you can . . ." She wanted to go to the Dutch border, to the county of
Bentheim, where her uncle was living. Father urged her to leave before the
baby arrived. So she told Hofmeier, and he went straight to Father and told
him, "If you say that one more time, I am going to report you. I will report
you!" Father wasn't supposed to say anything to the civilians! He wasn't supposed to tell anyone that it would soon be too late.*

I think my father organized a truck, a military vehicle of some kind, to take
some of our things. When we had first left Berlin in 1943, my parents thought
our house would be destroyed, so they had all the furniture, all the Oriental carpets—everything—moved to the castle. Now, less than two years later, there we
were again in a rush and we had to leave most of our belongings behind. But,
if I'm not mistaken, the stove was moved. It was a very important piece of furniture. Imagine moving a heavy gas stove through the snow—remember it was
the middle of winter—and onto a truck.

He also took Grandmother and me to Frankfurt an der Oder and put us on
a train back to Berlin. The trains were dangerously overcrowded; everyone was

bad-tempered. There was no civility left, and people were riding on the roofs—a practice that persisted even after the war.

My mother, Gisela, and Jürgen followed a few days later. They barely got out of there before the Russians reached Bottschow.

Jürgen once described just how precarious their situation had been to my wife, Mary Ellen.

We were literally running for our lives. When we arrived at the train station in Frankfurt an der Oder, I went ahead and got the tickets.

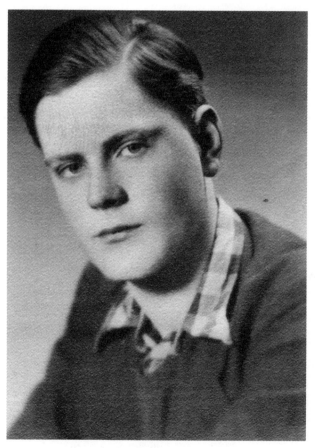

My brother, Jürgen, at age 14, 1943.

But there weren't any more trains, and all these people were freezing on the platform. Finally, a train came that was a hospital train of wounded German soldiers coming from the front. When it stopped, the people rushed to board but were held back. Everyone was told, "No, no, no." Then a door opened a bit, and I just muscled my way on; I grabbed my mother and sister and pulled them onto the train. Later, we learned that the people who were still at the Schloss [castle] had been murdered. The Russians had burst right in, raped and murdered, and then they set the place on fire.

We returned to our house—still standing, but badly damaged—in Spandau for about two or three weeks. I hardly have any recollections of our stay. It was close to the end of the war, in the late winter.

A short time after that we went to Kalbe, a town about sixty kilometers west of Berlin. A high school classmate of my mother was the wife of a local physician, and she and her husband had arranged for us to find refuge in a minister's house—the Protestant minister's house.

It was a very hectic time. Very little was normal. My father, of course, was gone, and my brother was now sixteen years old. At fifteen, boys were supposed to be drafted. But Jürgen was savvy. He knew that the war was lost, so he basically avoided the Nazis by not registering with the local police station when we went back to Berlin, nor when we moved to Kalbe. (Registering your name was a national requirement; it wasn't a Nazi directive but had been a long-established regulation. And, during the war, it made it easy for the Nazis to find the fifteen-year-olds who hadn't yet been drafted.) My brother never got drafted; he stayed out of the war. And we learned that he wasn't the only one—in Berlin draft evasion was rampant.

Of course, at the time, I had no idea what my brother was up to. I knew my mother was very concerned about him; after all, she needed my brother with Father away. He stepped up to the plate and took on the role of the adult male in our family; he took on a lot of responsibility. He wasn't only the oldest child, but he also already looked like an adult, standing six-foot-six tall.

In Kalbe, my mother sent me to school right away. It wasn't as traumatic as it had been in Leipzig, but even so it was still difficult. Almost overnight, we had gone from a very bucolic place to our home in Berlin, and then to this other town—where there was certainly no castle. We had gone from having acres of land to ourselves to being extremely crowded because the minister's house was full of other refugees, though I don't know where they came from.

On Sundays, I had to go to the local church, which was right across a small square. Afterward, I had to go back to the house with the minister, who let me count the collection money. (That, I actually enjoyed—that's why I remember it!) Even though it probably wasn't much, for an eight-year-old it was a lot—I had never seen so many coins and bills in one spot.

Kalbe, like Bottschow, was peaceful because the Germans had basically withdrawn most of their soldiers from the Western front to fight the Russians. (That January, the Russians were already near the Oder River, about thirty miles east of Berlin; it took them until April to get to Berlin. So there was *a lot* of fighting on the Eastern Front. On the Western Front, there was much less.)

However, one day I was on a country road and saw two fighter planes engaged in a battle. It was pretty amazing. I couldn't figure out which plane was German. They were shooting at each other, circling directly over my head. And then, all of a sudden, one of them went up in flames and—*pfffsh*—plunged into a field only a mile or so away. Since I had never heard about any German losses, I assumed that the German plane had shot down the enemy. But when I ran to the field to see what had happened, I saw it was the German plane that had been destroyed, and, of course, the pilot had been killed. The police was already there, and they wouldn't let me get very close. I was shocked—it was the first time that I had seen actual combat!

After the war ended, the Elbe River became the line between East Germany and West Germany. Where we were—just to the east of the Elbe—eventually became the Soviet zone. But the Soviets never conquered that area. The Americans initially reached the Elbe and then crossed it—one night, they rolled through Kalbe without a shot being fired.

My mother reported that there was a discussion among the townspeople about whether there should be resistance. She thought that was insane and said, "Let's not do this." At that point, people became much more outspoken; they shouted down the local Nazis, who had lost any clout. Order broke down. The people said, "We just want this to be over."

We were instructed to go to our cellars, because no one knew what the Americans would do, and we were afraid they might burn down all the houses. It was nighttime, dark, and we heard the rumble of tanks on the street nearby. My brother said, "I'm going to go outside, I want to see this." My mother said, "Under no circumstances. Under no circumstances." But my brother did whatever he wanted to. So he left. My mother was hysterical. After quite a while, he came back. He had a big smile on his face, and he said, "You want some chewing gum?" He had talked to the American soldiers. (Jürgen actually spoke English fairly well, having learned it in school.) The GIs were pretty friendly, he said, even though they had most certainly seen some horrible stuff. They didn't shoot at him or anything. He asked them, "Are you going to Berlin?" And they said, "Yeah, we're going to Berlin." They didn't know that they were not allowed to go that far. They could have been in Berlin the next day, but Eisenhower said, "No. Under the Yalta Agreement, the Russians will take Berlin." And so the Americans stopped.

Gisela also remembered the Americans occupying the town.

They greeted everybody very cheerfully. One of them gave me a gold ring. It was a wedding band. It also had an engraving. And he gave me a china cake plate with a kind of zigzag border. Blue and white. So I brought it to Mother. And she said, "He stole that from somewhere. It wasn't his." And she told me not to be so friendly; they didn't deserve that.

During this time, I also saw black soldiers for the first time. A friend and I had built a hut in the forest out of branches. It turned into a real little house with an opening for a window. One day, we heard voices and we looked out the window and saw two black men walking toward our hut. I remember thinking, Here comes the devil personified. *And so they came in and saw us children sitting there. And one of them said, "Nice here. Waips?"*

I only understood "waips." But he meant weapons. "No, no. Nothing." We didn't have anything on us of course. We had made everything by hand. And then he said again, "It's nice here." And they left. We never imagined blacks to be like that. So that finally erased the picture of the black man as the evil man, right?

A couple of days later, there were two American tanks parked on the square. Then they pulled out, heading west, and the British came.

Suddenly, there were British tanks and British military vehicles. I saw soldiers in skirts for the first time—Scottish soldiers in kilts. They were doing their thing, taking care of their equipment; Kalbe was just a way station for them. They weren't paying any attention to the civilians.

As for the local Nazi leaders, they essentially blended in and disappeared. There was no government at that point. Food was becoming harder and harder to find. The regular supply of provisions had ceased even before the Allies arrived. You had to have "connections" to get what you needed. We were more fortunate than others because my brother worked for a farmer who gave him milk and other farm products. Basically, the whole economy had collapsed into a barter system. I think Jürgen may have also helped another farmer's kids with their studies, and in exchange, he received more food.

Starvation was rapidly becoming a growing problem—particularly for the refugees who wound up in shelters in big cities, where they were completely dependent on other people in order to eat. There just wasn't any food. We were lucky in the sense that we went from one farming community to another.

Germany signed the capitulation in early May, officially marking the end of the war in Europe. And with it came a huge relief.

Of course, for us in Kalbe, the war had been over a few weeks earlier. Soon afterward, during the ensuing period of chaos, groups of Communists gained control. The Soviets knew that Kalbe was going to be in their zone; they had very carefully plotted out the Communist cells and who would be in charge of the various towns.

One day, printed announcements showed up everywhere, posted on lampposts and public buildings, saying that the real liberators were now coming. They said that the Soviet Liberation Army was arriving the following morning at 11 o'clock, and that they wanted the population to welcome them with flowers. Nobody had said that about the British and the Americans. We laughed. We *really* laughed about it—even then. It was so ridiculous. Who would welcome them with flowers? I mean, the war was over. We were disappointed that the British hadn't stayed, especially since everybody knew about the Russians' reputation.

The Russians' war with Germany had been brutal; they had raped and pillaged their way into Germany. That was well known—Propaganda Minister Joseph Goebbels made the most of it—and it became one of the things that motivated German troops to fight really hard against the Russians. Of course, the Russians only did to the Germans what the Germans had done to them, but that was not generally known in Germany.

So, when the Russians arrived, I went out—but not with flowers; I simply went out to take a look. And I found a completely disheveled bunch of soldiers. I could not believe that it was the Soviet occupying force. Their uniforms were dirty; their boots were dirty. They had horse-drawn wagons. Compared with the Americans and the British—who were all "spit and polish and everything new"—they looked like people from the Middle Ages. It was so dramatic, the difference between the troops. Nevertheless, there were some townspeople with flowers.

The Russians settled, I guess, in barracks that had formerly been used by the Germans. We heard that they didn't even know what running water was—in those days most places in Russia didn't have modern plumbing. The rumor was that they drank out of toilets because they thought this was the source of the water supply.

We were formally now in the Soviet Zone.

Gisela looked back on those tumultuous days and recalled our mother's strength and forthrightness.

We still had money. In Kalbe they were distributing refugee funds and Mother declined. She said, "I don't want to take any. We are in the lucky position of having enough money. Give it to somebody who really needs it." She also went to the bank or to the authorities to apply for a Lore [a small open train wagon] to transport all the goods—food and silver, a bale of silk from France, and whatnot, that the farmer Bahrs in Kalbe had given us—back to Berlin. And the official in charge told her, "That's a good idea, but Lores are only available for the most urgent things." Then he said, "But it's up to me to decide. You gave us money for the weakest of the weak and now we can return the favor. I'll get you your Lore."

Jürgen followed the train all the way to Magdeburg, about fifty kilometers away. And then he lost sight of it. When he got there in the morning, it was no longer there. The train had left—hopefully headed for Berlin. He didn't know. Once we were home in the fall of 1945, we waited a long time for it—how long I don't remember. Mother finally said, "Oh well, it was worth trying to get everything back to Berlin. We've lost so many things."

But, one day, we got a phone call from the railroad company. They had the Lore; it had arrived at the freight yard in Spandau. Mother went to Gatow, where she knew a farmer who had a carriage. She bribed him— she offered him good money. The man went and picked it up. And when he saw all the food—a whole sack of potatoes, imagine in those days, and rice, a whole sack, a few bags of flour, and I don't know what else . . .preserves and so on—he got big eyes and just stared. He told Mother, "You know what, my dear, what you offered me isn't enough. You're going to have to add a little something, otherwise I'm not driving the load!" Mother knew he wouldn't accept more money, and offered him the bale of silk instead. "Hmmm, okay," he said, "I like that idea. For that I'll drive it."

So Mother was pretty clever. She could bargain. She told us, "I didn't have any use for the silk anymore anyway." And that's how we got everything home. That was our great advantage that first year (after the war).

Well, there are so many stories that I know. After losing the train in Magdeburg, Jürgen returned to Kalbe to help prepare for our departure. He and Mother headed back to Berlin before us. They were on a train, which had stopped when they got to the American Sector because there was a 10 p.m. curfew. Mother had diarrhea. Can you imagine that? There she was sitting on a bench. And she said, "Jürgen, I can't get up."

Mother said, crying, "If I stand up now, it will all go into my pants. And I don't have anything clean with me. What do we do?"

And so they got off the train and walked across the tracks toward a house they had seen on the other side that had some lights on. When they got there, they saw that it was a NAAFI (Navy, Army and Air Force Institutes) club. They had those all over Germany for the Allies. The clubs were kind of recreation centers. So Mother and Jürgen went in because the doors were open. Nobody was there. Mother called out in English, "Hello? Hello?" Then a soldier came down the stairs, unarmed, just like that. You can imagine his surprise, right?

Mother was standing there, totally dirty and leaning on Jürgen. The soldier understood the situation and said, "A moment, please. A moment, please." He came back with a pile of towels and showed Mother to the bathroom and said, "Here, take it." Afterward, Mother basically put all her wet clothes back on. That didn't matter. Most importantly, they were a bit cleaner. She said it was horrible. The soldier returned just as she had finished. Jürgen was still standing or sitting in the outer room. The soldier was carrying a big tray with black tea. He said, "Come with me." They followed him into another room, and he said, "This is my room. I'm here the whole night. But I don't need it. You can sleep here. But at 5 o'clock I'll knock at the door and you must go, because others will be arriving."

What he did was strictly forbidden. In the morning, he quickly made them some more tea. And then they were on their way. They could have been shot, the two of them! Mother said, "Later, I wrote to so many places to see if I could track down that soldier. I really would have liked to thank him properly."

As for my father, after he helped arrange for us to leave Bottschow, January of '45, he went back to Berlin, and back to Tempelhof Airport, where he had been working before the war for Lufthansa. He was in charge of making sure the flights were going in and out—military flights, not commercial. Since it was toward the end of the war, a lot of Nazis—high-ranking Nazis—were escaping (unbeknownst to most people) and going west to the Alps or to Bavaria or someplace else, like South America.

Then the Battle of Berlin started. My father was there. German preparations started in March of '45, and the battle itself began in late April and lasted for about two weeks. It went street by street, almost, and was brutal. It soon became clear that Tempelhof was lost; the commander of Tempelhof Airport killed himself. (Suicide was very common in those days.) Apparently, he had been a fairly prominent Nazi. By default, my father had to take over, and he turned the airport over to the Russians. The exchange was fairly terse. My father said to the Russians, "I am representing Lufthansa. I am an aircraft engineer"—which they already knew. They said, "Fine."

By the way, the Soviet officers—unlike the troops—for the most part, were better educated, better behaved than many American officers. They almost all spoke relatively good German. And when they occupied villas they treated the places reasonably well.

They took my father, put him up in a villa, and said, "Would you like to work for us? We need German aircraft engineering skills." They explained, "Look, Berlin is destroyed; Germany is finished. We will move you and your family to Moscow. Give you a nice apartment. And you work for us."

Of course, they knew that the Americans had also gotten a lot of the German engineers. So they wanted to have their share.

My father said no. He refused to do that. He didn't want to work for the Soviets. Instead, he became a prisoner of war.

Even today, historians wonder what led relatively "ordinary" Germans to join the Nazi party and remain loyal to it after all was lost.

This is what I know about my own father. He became a member of the party in 1932—that was shortly before Hitler came to power. A few years ago, we were able to get a copy of his registration card from the Nazi archives in Berlin.

Father's Nazi membership registration card.

It carries the number 866,919. All Nazi membership cards were consecutively numbered. His was already a high number, but millions more joined subsequently. I believe he joined largely because of his career, but he was also politically naive. He was happy with Hitler, who basically told people to ignore the Versailles Treaty, and that Germany was going to build aircrafts again, commercial aircrafts, and soon military ones as well. Lufthansa had been losing money, but Hitler ordered massive infusions of cash into the aircraft industry and used Lufthansa as his main vehicle to do so.

Mother told Gisela—after she herself had become an adult—that in part Father had been forced to join.

Mother said he didn't want to join—not yet. But if you had a leading position at Lufthansa, you could only stay there if you had the party card in your pocket.

The fact that he joined the Nazi Party before Hitler came to power might simply mean that Father had been influenced by Erhard Milch, a big Nazi. Milch was a good friend, and Father did whatever Milch said. He was the one who got Father the Lufthansa post, and he probably pressured him. I imagine him saying, "If you want the post . . ." After the war, Milch sat in prison, in Wehrl, under the English for four years. And then he was released. The day he came out there was a Mercedes in front with keys and a check to get him started. He still had his friends somewhere! And for many years there were still those kinds of cliques that would help one another quietly, very hush- hush.

Of course Father joining the party was advantageous for his career. "Germany, Germany above all" were the lines in the song. Lufthansa was part of that, too. They wanted to join with other countries . . . not to exploit them, but to expand in order to expand technology, business. The floodgates had been opened in all sectors. But as Mother said, you could only keep your position at Lufthansa as long as you had the party card in your pocket. That was the condition. Otherwise you would get pushed to the side right away.

My father—like so many others—also believed that Hitler was a guy who was standing up for Germany.

The Führer often referred to the Treaty of Versailles as a "humiliation" of the German people. According to the treaty, in addition to Germany's demilitarization, Germany had to concede a number of territories and "admit full responsibility for starting the war." Today, historians generally agree that it was a bad treaty that helped the Nazis come to power in '32. It was the wrong thing to do and it was not repeated after World War II. Almost from the first day that Hitler took control, he worked toward a vast rearmament. In March of 1936, he reoccupied the Rhineland, while the Western powers did nothing about it.

So there was a general feeling at the time, which my father shared, that Hitler was the right man to lead Germany back on the right track. The nation also had started re-developing economically—full employment; the infrastructure was improved; Autobahns were built. And Lufthansa became a powerful airline. That was all good for my father, for his job, and for his career.

My father was a proud German; his feelings about the regime were very basic and personal, fundamental, and pragmatic. However, he was just one among millions who felt Hitler vindicated their collective feelings about the Versailles Treaty. He never became a Nazi official; he was an ordinary party member. Anyone could join the Nazi Party. Does that excuse him? Of course not.

When my father refused the Soviets' offer, they sent him first to Buchenwald, which had been one of the big concentration camps. The prisoners had been liberated. Now it was filled with German prisoners of war. Although he was an officer, he volunteered to work—officers, according to the Geneva Convention, could not be forced to work. They put him on the night shift to aid in burying fellow prisoners of war, who had died of diseases or malnutrition.

After a few months, they sent him to Russia, though we did not know any of this. For two years, we didn't know whether he was alive or dead. Then the first postcard arrived. It was pretty exciting. The prisoners were apparently allowed to write one postcard a month. I'm not sure why it took so long for us to receive a postcard, but perhaps it had to do with transportation. After all, everything had been destroyed. Anyway, he may have written ten cards, and none of them were delivered. But suddenly, with this first card, we learned that he was alive.

Postcard from Father, Siberia, 1947 (front and back).

He didn't say much in those cards. My mother was also allowed to write one card a month, and we kids were allowed to write. It was an effort for me to write something worthwhile—he was just too far removed from our lives. I don't know how many of our notes he actually received. There would be long breaks between each of the cards. Five, six months would pass during which we heard nothing. Then a postcard would arrive and we could see that he was in a different camp. The reason we knew this is that each camp had a number that was written on the postcard. I think there were only thirty or forty cards during the entire five-year period that he was in Russia.

I remember, one time, two men came to the house. This was maybe '47 or '48. They said that they had been together with my father in a prison in Siberia and that they had a way of getting food and supplies to him. Even though we were in dire straits as well, my mother gave them as much as possible. Later we learned that it was all a hoax. They were swindlers, "confidence men" preying on the women who were sitting at home, waiting for their husbands to return—this was pretty typical of that time.

FOUR

AT WAR'S END

We were still in Kalbe when we found out from the newspapers that Berlin was to be divided into four sectors, and that our house would be in the British sector. So, obviously, we wanted to get back to Berlin.

Today, you can go from Kalbe to Berlin in less than two hours. In 1945, it took us probably the entire day. There was train service, but it was only running irregularly. The trains were very crowded and it probably was a huge hardship—I don't really remember much else aside from the crowding.

When we came home, we discovered our house was full of people. Berlin had been bombed out, and people had moved into any structure where they could find a room. The city was under military occupation, but clearly they had used local authorities to assist with locating housing for those who had lost everything. Those local officials gave preference to anti-Nazis, and our house had been taken over by several anti-Nazi families. Although they realized that it was our house, they were not about to move. Though I don't remember any particulars, I'm sure there were some less-than-pleasant exchanges between my mother and the people living in her home.

A close family friend, whom I knew as Uncle Hugo, came to our aid. We didn't see him all that much, but after the war—in the period that my father was away—he was always there when it mattered. Uncle Hugo kind of instinctively knew when we needed some help here and there. He had real credentials, because he himself was an anti-Nazi; everybody knew that. He got away with that because he was a veteran who had lost the bottom part of both legs during World War I. Even the Nazis wouldn't mess with him.

I should mention that Uncle Hugo actually wasn't my uncle; my siblings and I just called him "uncle" as he was a very close friend of our father's. His full name was Hugo Thienhaus. He was a real estate developer and by the time we returned to Berlin he was already getting orders to start rebuilding the city up from the rubble; in fact, over time he became the largest, or one of the largest, private builders in Berlin. He had money and would help us financially as best as he could. He also helped us to move back into the house. I don't know how he did it, but he got the squatters to make room for us. Perhaps, some allowance was made for the fact that my father was presumed to be a prisoner of war, and there was now his wife, a single mother with three children.

Gisela remembered Uncle Hugo used to tell our mother "If I hadn't met Erika (Mother's best friend who shared the same name) then I would have taken you." He may have been joking, but my sister agreed that he was a big help to Mother.

I think they liked each other a lot. At least he didn't abandon her during the war. When asked, he was always ready to help.

He was the biggest critic of Hitler that we had in our family, from the moment Hitler came to power. And when the adults got together he always would say, "You don't know what you are doing." He knew more! He always knew more about what was going on in the background. I am sure he had also read Mein Kampf *all the way through. So he knew a lot more. And they didn't want to hear about it, neither my father's other close friend Eberhard Kranz—who was a fanatic Nazi—nor Father.*

In spite of all this, they remained friends before, during, and after the war because they were three intelligent people who could also talk about other things. They would simply leave politics out of their conversation.

Uncle Hugo was incredibly important to me as long as he lived. He was a much more practical mentor than my parents ever were. Not only had he helped out during the difficult years after the war, but I could also look up to him because he had diagnosed and avoided the Nazi curse.

The winter of '45 was very difficult. It was almost worse than any time during the war—if anything can be worse than war. The German people were completely demoralized. In Berlin alone, thousands of people starved or froze to death. Our house was equipped for central heating; the heating source was coal, or coke—a coal derivative. So we had a coal cellar with a boiler. But we couldn't afford to run it because there was not enough coal; instead we used only a stove in our living room. We would all gather around it to try to stay warm. This was true of every household—everyone had their own little heating area.

I was constantly hungry and went to bed hungry every night. My brother occasionally went out to the country on the train; he would take silver or whatever we had left in the house. Everybody did this. The city people bargained with the farmers to get whatever they could get—a chicken or eggs—whatever. The farmers all of a sudden had all the Oriental carpets that used to be in the city; the city people had nothing.

We also had ration cards—different from the ones we had had during the war. Under the general supervision of the British everything was new. The rations now were less—considerably less. You received a card for the whole month and the allotment was not enough to ever make you full, or even get you to the point where you no longer felt hungry. It was all based on bare necessities. On the first day of a ten-day period my brother would sometimes go and get his rations for the entire period, and eat it all immediately. My mother would cry endlessly. She would say of Jürgen, "What are we going to do with this sad boy now for the next nine days? He has already eaten everything." For the remaining nine days I don't know how he managed, but he always found more food. On his own initiative he would go out in the country and forage.

Jürgen was seventeen years old and still growing. Sometimes he would also snatch some of my food, which would make Mother really angry. And I would get angry. There would be times he and I would get into fistfights. Even though he was much bigger, I usually was the one to start the fight—and lose. I would get a bloody nose, and my mother would scream for us to stop. It could get really ugly.

My brother tried to be responsible, but when he was hungry he was something else. He would get up earlier than the rest of us, and whatever was in the pantry he would devour in minutes. Often, by the time I got up, there was nothing left for my breakfast. Of course he usually had already left for school before I realized what had happened. When he was around and I would complain and say something, he would say, "So what? What are you going to do about it? I am hungry, so I eat." It was very Darwinian. My sister did without as well. I think we dealt with it because we felt that Jürgen just needed more food than we did.

Gisela's memories of our hunger were also quite vivid.

One time, Mother went to see relatives and left us alone for a week. Her only worry for us was that there would be enough bread and butter, or, well, grease. So she cut three strips [of the grease ration] and made seven indentations in each. Everybody was to get their smidgen and some bread to go with it. And of course we had a huge appetite at the beginning and didn't really think much about the sections. By Wednesday we had eaten everything, Jürgen and I. But suddenly you came along with your stockpile and said, "Now I can lead the good life." I think we both wanted to kill you. We were amazed that you still had all of it. And then you laid the butter on thick right in front of our eyes. We really wanted to kill you (because we were always hungry).

Sometimes, Mother would go into the fields and pick orach. That's this kind of weed, with mealy leaves. Tastes better than spinach. She also heard that if you dissolve yeast and add a little milk, a little salt, a bit of marjoram, then you could make a paste that tasted like liverwurst. How often did we get that on bread! She would spread yeast paste on our bread.

Jürgen's appetite was insatiable. At my confirmation . . . this was 1947, very lean times . . . on my gift table was a loaf of bread. And Jürgen called me away from the guests and said, "I'm so hungry. I'll get you another loaf on the black market. Tomorrow. I can buy you another one. The theater [where he worked part time] still owes me money. So I can buy you one tomorrow. But give me this one today." And I thought, "Well, I guess nobody will notice." Also I didn't want to touch it yet. It was too precious.

So he went off to the kitchen, got himself a big pot of syrup and finished the whole loaf. Then he cleaned everything up and returned to our guests in the living room. "Oh," said Uncle Hugo, "I was starting to worry that we weren't going to get a chance to see you today." Jürgen didn't say a word. Didn't say, "Oh, I just ate all of your bread." Then Uncle Hugo said, "Listen, this bread that I gave Gisela, do you think you could eat it all in one sitting?" "I think so," was Jürgen's response. And Uncle Hugo said, "Well, come here and eat the whole loaf in front of me. And if you can finish the whole thing, I'll give you another one and Gisela will get a new one too, of course."

Now Jürgen didn't know what to do. He immediately went over to Mrs. Prediger, a neighbor, who traded on the black market, and she always had some bread—there was only one kind. And so he came back with the cutting board and the pot of syrup and put thin layers of syrup on slice after slice of bread. And he ate more than half. More than half. And there were about five or six slices to go when Jürgen started slowing down.

Then Uncle Hugo said, "Okay, let's be honest. A whole loaf of bread is a lot. Shall we spare you the rest?" And Jürgen said to Uncle Hugo, "Ask Gisela. That's my second loaf." They couldn't contain themselves. How someone could be so hungry, right?

Oh boy, could he eat!

In the course of her conversations with Marc Rosenwasser (Preface), who interviewed her as well, my wife, Mary Ellen, told him other stories that she had heard from my mother and brother about this period of extreme deprivation.

During the war and right after, Erika (Karl's mother) had to depend greatly on Jürgen. She was already doing everything she could—literally trying to keep her family out of the cold. She was a trouper. But under any other circumstances she shouldn't have put Jürgen in that situation, where she totally depended on him to keep the family alive. Though he was six and a half feet tall, he was still just a sixteen-year-old boy. And although he was physically able to do a lot and was bright and enterprising, he suffered under the responsibility. He always did the best he could, but he was never in the position to be able to take pride in his accomplishments. According to Jürgen, everything was so horrible that it was impossible for him to make it right. He never resented his mother for her dependence, though—and she adored him.

In the early sixties, while we were courting, Karl and I were separated for the better part of a year—ironically, he was in America and I was in Germany—and I got to know Karl's brother very well; Jürgen and I would sit around drinking wine and smoking cigarettes and he would tell me all kinds of stuff.

Something Jürgen talked about was how dreadfully malnourished everyone was right after the war, and how typhoid (or typhus) spread like wildfire through the city. Both Erika and Gisela contracted it and were in the hospital. And Ingolf (what Karl was known as back then) was sent on his bike to the family doctor in the neighborhood to get a shot—a vaccination. After he biked home, his leg started to hurt. He went to bed, and had terrible, terrible pain in his legs. Jürgen was at home and got the doctor to come over. The doctor ruled out polio, but he didn't know what to do; he thought that it could have been a reaction to the vaccine.

There was nothing to eat in the house, so the main thing that Jürgen had to do was to find some food. He went out and scrounged around; it took him almost the entire day. When he came home with what food he had managed to get by bartering, he could hear Ingolf upstairs still crying from the pain. Jürgen took the food out of his bag. But he said that he was so starved that he just went crazy and ate every single bit of it, every bit of it. And then he had to go upstairs and tell Ingolf that he just didn't have any luck finding food. When Jürgen told me this—I vividly remember, I was sitting in a nearby chair—he had tears in his eyes. He said, "That was one of the most horrible times of my whole life." He was never able to tell Ingolf what he had done. Jürgen was psychologically a very complicated guy, often incapable of expressing himself.

Since the doctor had no pain medication, Jürgen decided that he somehow had to get Ingolf to the hospital. It was snowing, and the only road that was passable was about a half mile away, so Jürgen ended up carrying Ingolf that distance. Imagine: Ingolf was nine years old, and Jürgen was very malnourished. But they made it to the main road and waited for any method of transportation to come by. They waited and waited, but nothing showed up. Finally, a three-wheeler (like a large motorized tricycle) came into view,

*and the driver agreed to let Jürgen put Ingolf in the back. However, after
a short distance, the vehicle became bogged down in the snow. He couldn't
make it to the hospital. Jürgen gathered up Ingolf, and somehow managed
to carry him back home.*

*Jürgen got word to his mother in the hospital. She later described to me how
she made it home on foot. Erika was so weak that she walked from one tree
to the next. She'd make it to a tree, hang on to a branch, gather her strength,
scope out the next tree, and make it to that tree. I don't know whether she
did that all the way from the hospital, or whether she found some sort of
transportation down to the road. The hospital was at least three miles away.
Everyone eventually recovered.*

The following spring and summer, in 1946, we converted the whole backyard
and front yard into spaces for growing things—seeds and animals we received
through bartering. We grew cabbage, other vegetables, and potatoes. We also
had fruit trees—pear, apple, plum, cherries—both sweet and sour cherries—and
walnut trees. We grew anything that would grow.

We had rabbits. And we had chickens. We knew we would have to kill them.
Downstairs, in the basement, Mother showed me how to do it. It was never very
pleasant; my mother would take a chicken and cut off its head. At first, it was difficult because we loved those chickens. We had given them names, and we knew
exactly how many eggs each of them laid. Yet, I remember that I was looking
forward to eating those chickens.

We also had a rooster, and once in a while the eggs would hatch. One day,
there was a whole bunch of cute little yellow chicks—then they were all gone.
They had gotten out of the enclosure, and magpies and other birds of prey must
have picked them off. That was a tragedy.

Again, hunger was our most pressing concern. The rabbits needed to be fed, too. They would have eaten grass but we had no lawn left. Not too far from our house, there were fields, which were essentially irrigation fields that were owned by the city; they had been there prior to the war. The sewage would go into canals and run through these fields; the odor was horrible, although it would dissipate over time. In between the canals, really beautiful tall grass grew. But we were not allowed to take any of that grass because it was needed for other purposes; there were even British soldiers protecting the fields with guns. So at night, under the cover of darkness, I would go and grab food for our rabbits. There were times when I heard shots being fired. The soldiers would shoot at people who trespassed, so I crawled on my belly through the stinking fields, pulled the grass, and shoved it into a burlap bag, then crawled back out, as if I were in the infantry. I was pretty terrified. But it got the adrenaline going, and I was pretty clever in those days. It was exciting, and I never got caught. That was good.

But even gardening was not easy. In our yard we had moles eating the potatoes, and we had to try to get rid of them. We could see them when they were moving earth beneath the surface, making tunnels. We would then go very quietly, barefoot: if the sun was shining, we would make sure that our shadows wouldn't fall on the mound, because the moles would immediately disappear. The moment when we saw a mole tunneling, we'd hit the spot with the spade, toss up the mole, and kill it. While the moles were eating the potatoes, the squirrels were eating our walnuts. I would shoot at them with an air rifle.

These were things that everybody did then. In hindsight, it all looks pretty callous, but when you are hungry, it becomes pretty basic. Life was a struggle. But I think it is human nature, and it certainly is true in my case, to want to suppress just how hard it actually was. There were also lighter moments.

I woke up one morning hearing loud laughter coming from my mother's bedroom next door. She was there with Gisela and told me that they had just counted all the money we had: It added up to seventy *Pfennig*—not even one *Mark*! They found that hilarious—gallows humor masking real desperation.

During the summer, when our garden produced fruits and vegetables, we sometimes took some of this produce to our local grocer's, hoping to exchange it for staples such as flour or sugar. One day, Gisela and I climbed up our sweet cherry tree, which had grown considerably during the war years since it had never been pruned, and we picked the ripe cherries. Gisela then carried the full basket to the store and presented it to the store's owner, Frau Dischereit. She looked at the cherries and was about to give us something in exchange, when I spoke up and said, "Don't buy these cherries, Frau Dischereit, they all have worms!" (Which was true.) I wish I could attribute my outburst to an early sign of my ethics and honesty, but I did it strictly to annoy my sister and prevent her from returning triumphantly to my mother. Frau Dischereit, it should come as no surprise, declined the offer of the cherries.

In those really dark days, after the war had ended, my mother started selling wool yarn out of our house to bring in some money. There were no stores where you could buy sweaters, so people would knit what they needed. Everything had to be done from scratch due to the deprivation. Yarn, however, was very hard to find. Luckily, the husband of my mother's sister—the former U-boat captain from Leipzig—who was now in Hamburg, was either the owner of or a senior person in a company that imported wool. He provided Mother with yarn, thank goodness, charging her only a modest amount, and the wool would come to us in bundles, wrapped in paper.

Customers would ring our doorbell—no advertising, it was all word of mouth. My mother was a fabulous saleswoman. We joked about it, because working as a retail saleswoman was somewhat below her normal standards. But she was very charming; she would sometimes offer the customers a cup of tea. And I would help her by going and getting the right wool. It came in different sizes and quantities and colors—although sometimes we didn't have in stock what people wanted.

We gave the business a fancy name, the Prussian Wool Manufacturing Company—it was never an official name—at which we laughed our heads off.

I thought the whole enterprise was neat, especially the chance to see my mother in action. As I said before, she had a great instinct for business. She came from a family of savvy entrepreneurs. She knew how to sell. Later on, as supplies became more plentiful, and as stores reopened with ready-made products, such home businesses died, though Mother's business foray ended for other reasons.

According to Gisela, Mother had started the wool business after her insurance investment was used up.

I believe it was '48. Mother had a little additional money. She had cashed out her annuity from the insurance company, Gehrling. And that's what we lived off of. And when that was used up, things got pretty tight. She started selling small amounts of wool. After school, I would go to the clinic Buttermann in Spandau to deliver the wool to the customers. But when the orders increased, Uncle Helmut told her he could no longer supply her. He said, "You have to do the trade exam." I remember she came home and said, "I need to take the trade exam. That's next week, on Saturday. This week I won't have any time for you, except in the case of an emergency. I'll make food, but otherwise please leave me alone as best as you can. I need to work. I need to work." That made me laugh.

She had already learned bookkeeping. But the exam covered everything about yarn, all the varieties, where they come from, and how they are produced. She took the exam and came home, "I got it, I got it!" She showed us her trade license. Now she was able to order as much wool as she wanted. And then, when things were really going well, we set up a wool shop in the kids' room. She didn't even knit herself. When people asked how to make a hat, Mother always said, "Let me write it down. Where do you live? Then I can send my daughter over and she will show you." I was already a champion knitter back then.

We were doing OK. And then father comes home from Siberia [in 1949], and he immediately put a stop to it. "My wife doesn't need to work." Mother said, "Let's keep it going for now, until we know how much you'll be making. Then we can still . . ." "No," he said, "I will not tolerate it. I will not tolerate it." Right away. Mother had to stop! Uncle Helmut didn't understand it either. Nobody understood. But Mother had to do it. Father was very dictatorial.

In the meantime, I had founded my own business. After the war, when I was nine years old, I started a newspaper and called it the *Berliner Kinderzeitung*, or the "*Berlin Children's Paper.*" The first issue was May 26th, 1946. I modeled the layout of my paper after *Der Tagesspiegel* (*The Daily Mirror*), which was the newspaper we received at home. Initially, I lettered it all by hand—all four pages. I even added a publisher's address. It was very formal.

Every day, I would spend one to two hours putting it together. I didn't write the articles. I would copy ones that I found interesting from other sources—such as books and newspapers. I'd make a separate page for adults and called it "*Für die Erwachsenen*" ("For the Grownups"). I still have a complete collection of all the newspapers I wrote.

I only would make one copy. After my family had read it, I would mail it to Uncle Hugo, who would regularly contribute to "Letters to the Editor," and he would forward it to other "uncles"—actual uncles—and my aunts in West Germany. How could they refuse a nine- or ten-year-old kid? They would generally send me a little bit more than the cost of the subscription. Initially, it probably went to just four or five people. Of course my brother had to read it, and my sister had to read it. And my mother. In the second issue I had a little place where you could renew your subscription. You had to sign your name and write your address. And write your date of birth!

Die Mücke

Die Mücke erscheint zu Beginn eines Monats und an besonderen Feiertagen. Bisher erschien im Dezember: „Das Jugendheft" Nr. 2 (nicht mehr vorhanden) und Nr. 3.

Nr. 21   Berlin, Weihnachten 1949   Sondernummer

1. Dezemberausgabe (der Mücke), 3. Jahrgang, sowie der „Mücke" Nr. 1   4. Zeitungsjahrgang

Er ist da!

Nach 4½ Jahren ist unser Vater aus der Gefangenschaft zurückgekehrt!

Damit es dem Gedächtnis erhalten bleibt, berichten wir kurz das Wichtigste.

Das Wichtigste wollen wir erwähnen, damit wir es uns immer wieder ins Gedächtnis zurückrufen können: Sonntag, 27. November, 1. Advent. Das „Kleeblatt" sitzt beim Adventskaffee. Durch Zufall bekommt es im Radio Namen von Berliner Heimkehrern zu hören. Als Spandau dran ist, ist er dabei! Verständlicherweise wurden alle...

[...]

Kleidung: Russische Mütze, dicke gelbe Wattejacke, dünne Hose, Wickelgamaschen, eine Art Schuhe. — Darunter eine dünne Monteurjacke und sonst war wirklich nicht viel mehr da. So genau habe ich das auch nicht gesehen. — Näheres in den nächsten Nummern. —

Over time, I started writing my own stuff and mimeographing the pages. The name of the paper was changed to *Die Mücke* (*The Mosquito*). I was at the Kant Gymnasium at that time, and its school newspaper was called *Die Hornisse* (*The Hornet*), and I thought that my paper should have a more modest title. I kept this up for about five years. It consumed an enormous percentage of my time.

For some three years after the war, we still lived among all those people in our house. But, by '48 or so, only one family remained, and we again had plenty of space in our house. We had become very friendly with that family; they liked us kids. Eventually, they started paying us rent. In the other little house on the property was another family who began paying us rent, as well.

At home in Berlin, 1949.

Little by little, everything returned to normal; things started to improve, positive things, in '47, early '48. It seemed like almost every day there would be a little bit of good news. Ice cream, for example, was suddenly available—at least on occasion. The schools got a supply of schoolbooks, and printed books started to reappear. There was paper to write on.

A bridge in the city that had been blown up was repaired and you could walk or ride the streetcar across that bridge again, which would save you twenty minutes in your travels. I would read the newspapers and see these little stories about the progress. I think the Allies were behind those papers, trying to boost the morale of the population.

Each armed service had its own local radio stations, which we could all listen to: the British had the British Forces Network (BFN), and we began to listen—primarily for the music, but also to try to learn some English; the American Forces Network (AFN) also had a huge draw; then the French had their own; and the Russians had theirs. Three languages, in perfect clarity, on every radio—plus of course the German stations. The best-known station in Berlin was Radio in the American Sector (RIAS), which we could hear in the British sector as well. Although it broadcast in German, it was essentially an American-sponsored radio station.

So the mood gradually picked up.

People began having enough to eat. Nobody was getting fat, of course, but what we ate was healthful—no junk food. In hindsight that was possibly a good thing; cases of diabetes and obesity were rare.

Then the Berlin blockade took place, and we were back in the dumps in West Berlin.

FIVE

EAST MEETS WEST

After the war, Germany had been divided into four zones—Soviet, American, British, and French. Berlin was located deep in the Soviet Zone, but, under the Four Power Agreement struck at Yalta, it was itself divided into four sectors, one for each of the occupying forces. Thus American, British, and French forces were stationed in the middle of the Soviet Zone. That part of Berlin was called West Berlin. The Soviet sector was called East Berlin. West Berlin was like a Western island behind the Iron Curtain—a term that Churchill coined. Similarly, the three western zones in the rest of Germany came to be called West Germany, and the Soviet Zone was called East Germany. West Berlin became an outpost of West Germany inside East Germany. To travel between West Germany and West Berlin, you had to cross through East German territory.

The Four Power Agreement called for Berliners to have no travel restrictions between the four sectors. The streetcars, the buses, the subways, and the elevated trains, all went back and forth, in and out, and around. There was mobility among the populace. I was a soccer fan and had a favorite team that played in the Berlin League. I rode my bicycle to every game—home and away—and several of them took place in East Berlin. Some of the commuter trains even went outside of Berlin, and you could ride them anytime. The only restrictions were at the borders between West Berlin and East Germany, and East and West Germany. But the standards of living and the degree of reconstruction between the three Western sectors and the Soviet sector began to diverge noticeably, with the Western sectors pulling ahead.

Traveling between the different sectors was quite interesting for other reasons, as well. Because each sector had a lot of military personnel in uniform, you always knew when you crossed from one into another. As I mentioned, we were in the British sector, and we had a lot of British soldiers. They rode on regular public buses and public transportation, and were often intoxicated and very loud. The Americans used their own vehicles; I don't think their soldiers were allowed to use public transportation. The French sector was the smallest, and the one I went into the least; it was to the north of us, and I seldom had a reason to go there.

We had minimal interaction with the British soldiers in our sector. Fraternization with civilians was not encouraged by the military authorities in any of the sectors—and few Germans spoke English in those days. We saw them as occupiers, but in a more benign sense; we accepted the fact that we were now under military occupation. The British pretty much dismantled the steel factories and other industrial plants and moved whatever they could use to Britain. The Germans, however, had great respect for the Americans because the Americans never dismantled any industry.

As for the Soviet sector, the military were also quite visible, mostly riding around in military vehicles. All their elite units were in East Berlin. Being there was their crowning achievement. But it became clearer and clearer that the reconstruction was proceeding faster in West Berlin than in East Berlin. The Russians rebuilt some showplaces, but you could see that the general population was worse off. Between '45 and '48 an outflow of East Germans into the West had already begun.

What I started to notice, in about 1947, was the attempt of the Western Allies to make West Berlin's standard of living equal to that of West Germany. Berlin was supposed to have been managed by a military council from the four powers, whose job it was to administer the whole city in a uniform way. This failed increasingly because of Soviet intransigence. The Soviets' objective was to absorb the Western sectors into their own sector; they viewed the Western sectors as intruders inside the Russian zone. West Berlin was an island of prosperity in an otherwise miserable East German country.

West Germany, meanwhile, had become the Federal Republic of Germany (FRG). In response, East Germany became the German Democratic Republic (GDR), a Soviet puppet state.

A major blow to the Four Power Agreement, under which Berlin was supposed to be governed, was the currency reform of 1948 in which the *Reichsmark* was retired in West Germany and a new currency introduced—the *Deutsche Mark*. The Western Allies decided to include West Berlin in that reform, over the objections of the Soviets.

Every citizen received sixty Deutsche Marks from the government; that's all they got. But, immediately, things started appearing in the stores. It was the beginning of what was called the "German Miracle." From that time on, progress in the western regions was immense and rapid.

In response, the Soviets and their East German puppets did two things. First, they introduced their own new currency, which they called the *Mark*—not the Deutsche Mark, but just the Mark. From day one, the Mark traded on the black market for one-quarter of the value of the Deutsche Mark. The introduction was a flop because they didn't have the economic progress that was taking place in West Germany. Second, the Soviets decided, enough is enough, as they decided to find a way to absorb West Berlin.

It's important to remember that all traffic—trains, trucks, barges, and so on—had to travel from West Germany through East Germany to reach West Berlin. So, under the pretense of saying that there were mechanical problems, etc., on June 15, 1948, the Soviets denied access to anyone coming from the West; they closed this and that route, and finally everything was closed—except the airways. At that point, the Allies, under the leadership of President Truman and the US commander General Lucius Clay, decided that they would try to supply West Berlin through the air.

We were horrified by what was going on. No one really expected that a city of 2.2 million people could be kept alive by air. We considered leaving for West Germany—initially there were still some commercial airline flights—but we couldn't afford that; it was out of the question. And, if we did leave, where would we go? We were stuck, along with all the other people.

The Russians said to the West Berliners, "We will sign you up for East Berlin ration cards." They were worse than what we were used to having—but better than what we were going to have. It was quite an incentive. But there was a *quid pro quo*, i.e., you had to sign a petition that you wanted to be part of "Greater (Communist) Berlin." I think only about two percent of the population took advantage of that. That, in itself, showed the Western powers that West Berliners really didn't want to be stuck behind the Iron Curtain.

When the blockade started, the biggest problem was supplying the electric utilities with coal—they were all coal-fueled—and later on, in the winter, supplying coal to heat the houses. Thus, the immediate effect of the Soviets closing off West Berlin was that power outages occurred. In Germany, however, nothing stays out of control for very long, and the local authorities quickly took hold of the situation. They decided Berlin needed power during the day to keep industry, businesses and public transportation running. (People still went to work.) The Allies started flying in coal at that point, but it wasn't nearly enough.

Almost everybody in West Berlin got only two hours of electricity in a twenty-four-hour period—that was in the middle of the night, like from one to three, or from two to four. Everybody got up. During those two hours they cooked a meal, did the laundry, or did whatever needed power. The rest of the day, there was no power to households.

In our community, we got lucky. Our power was supplied by an East German utility company because we were less than a kilometer from the border that ran between West Berlin and East Germany. (You might say we were so far west that we were east!) And the East German power company never cut off our power. Maybe they didn't realize that some of it went to a small West Berlin enclave.

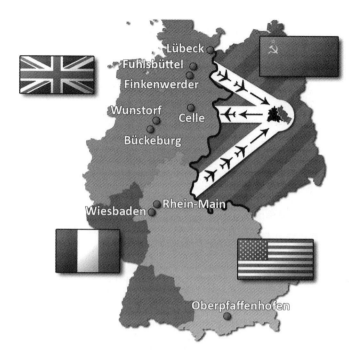

Allied air corridors, the Berlin Airlift, 1948-1949.

Food was, of course, a different story. Although the shortage of food was much worse in the immediate aftermath of the war, fears of starvation were renewed and lasted throughout the airlift. We were part of the West Berlin food supply, and again we were on very tight rations. Nothing was fresh anymore. Everything that was flown in was dried: powdered milk, powdered potatoes, and even powdered carrots. There were virtually no fresh vegetables. That was, of course, a setback. We all knew that every effort was being made to keep us alive, but nobody knew how long the blockade would last and if the airlift could be maintained.

The airlift was primarily carried out by the Americans, because they had the most planes. But the British were very active. It completely changed everything for the Berliners. No one could believe that the Allies had decided to organize this airlift. Everybody expected the Allies to say, "Well, Berlin, you know, let's just get rid of it." And that is what a lot of the people said in Washington and Paris and London. But when they did decide to go through with the airlift—I think thanks mainly to President Truman—they said, "We will stand on principle here; we have our forces stationed there. We are not going to walk out." The fact that there were military personnel stationed in the three Western sectors made it less likely that they would cave in.

The Cold War had started.

Stories began to appear in both the American and British press about the bravery of the Berliners for having rejected the offer from the Communists, and all that. In an instant, we felt that we had gone from being the villains to being the heroes. That turned the Berliners' sentiment toward the Allies into real admiration. It was a complete turnaround, very dramatic.

In the Western sectors of Berlin, the Allies still controlled the newspapers. But for the first time, the German papers' publishers introduced editorials—even though there were limits to how critical one could be of the military authorities. Nevertheless, it was clear that the Western Allies were trying to put Western Germany back on its feet, and start a democratic tradition before pulling out. They did not want to repeat what had happened in Versailles.

There were efforts to help the population. In '47, the Marshall Plan kicked in—an American initiative of about $130 billion of US aid to Europe. It was the exact opposite of what Versailles had been. If it hadn't been for the Marshall Plan, who knows what would have happened, because the Communist propaganda was very, very strong in Western Europe, pushing the story that everything the Soviet Union was doing was heroic, etc. (As a matter of fact, in Italy—and in France, I think—the Communists won some elections.) The Marshall Plan helped eventually to discredit the Communists.

Through the summer and particularly the fall of '48, we worried whether the airlift could drop enough supplies to get us through the winter. "In the winter," the Russians said, "you're not going to make it with this airlift." That scared all of us. We anxiously watched the daily number of flights and the daily tonnage. Every day, that was the most important piece of news. Contrary to during the war, now the constant airplane noise overhead was welcome. I remember literally waking up one night, in a cold sweat, because it was so quiet. No planes. When I looked out the window, it was foggy and the planes couldn't fly. We lost hundreds of flights, and we fell further behind. But, at that point, they had cranked up the airlift. On top of everything else, they built a third airport, Tegel, after flying in cement and everything to build it in approximately four months. So that allowed for even more flights.

A British Sunderland seaplane during the airlift.

The airlift was, for me as a twelve-year-old kid, very important. All those planes were coming in, and one of the airports the Allies used—besides Berlin's Tempelhof—was Gatow; the one close to us, in the British sector. Mostly British planes landed there, but that later changed to include American planes. And almost immediately after the start of the blockade, seaplanes also landed on the Havel River directly in front of our house, which I thought was terribly exciting, though they took off farther down the river. They cleared that section of the Havel of all sailboats and other sorts of watercraft. The seaplanes were called Sunderlands. There weren't that many planes that landed, but on each flight they brought in up to five tons of supplies. I remember watching them from our bedroom; they made big waves when they landed.

I was still publishing my little newspaper, and I made a "special edition," a book really, seventeen or eighteen pages long; I called it *Airlift Mücke*. In that special edition, I included pictures that I drew of the planes, such as the Sunderland, the DC4, and the Skymaster (which carried up to nine tons), as well as—I don't know why—a map of Denmark. I also included a running chart for the duration of the airlift with information taken from the daily newspapers. The chart consisted of five columns: the number of days into the airlift, the date, the number of flights, the total tonnage (of supplies) delivered that day, and comments. For example, January 20, 1949, I jotted down: "Tobacco for Berlin;" the next day: "Russian fighters practice over Berlin;" and the day after that: "25,000 tons of coal" (thus far in the winter). Then, 23 January 1949: "More Russian exercises in the corridor. A Dakota (a DC3) with 22 passengers, including 17 children, crashes and they all died." (They would sometimes fly German children out of Berlin to West Germany to live with relatives or to get them medical help.). Then, 30 January 1949: "71,960 tons is a new record for a month."

My friends and I would regularly bicycle over to the Gatow airport. There was a fence, but you could still get pretty close. I thought it was just amazing to see planes landing every two minutes—taking off and landing. As soon as the planes stopped, the doors opened and stuff came out. For a kid, witnessing that was fantastic. I had never felt like a villain, but I felt that Germans must be inferior to have lost the war and have all the foreign troops around. Yet, in that moment, watching the planes, I felt that we were at the center of the universe.

When the airlift first started it was poorly organized. The US Government had to bring mothballed planes over from the States. One of the American pilots was Colonel Gail Halvorsen, who came to be known as the "Candy Bomber" because he would drop candies to us kids. He flew a Skymaster over from Kansas or someplace, all the way to Frankfurt am Main.

Airlift statistics for January 1949.

C-54 Douglas Skymaster piloted by Gail Halvorsen, releasing small parachutes with candy during the Berlin Airlift.

Gail Halvorsen, the "Candy Bomber," 1940s.

I am not exactly sure at what point the Colonel started dropping these parachutes with candies, but when that news came out everyone was excited. Candy, of course, was not something that they had been flying in for the population. And word of it immediately drew huge crowds of kids to Tempelhof Airport. Tempelhof was in the middle of Berlin—pretty far away from where we lived. However, a few times I got on my bike and rode there. We would stand on heaps of rubble from the war, which allowed us to overlook the airfield and watch the glide path of the airplanes—a tough approach, with buildings on both sides.

Halvorsen's commander had given him permission to drop the candy, then other soldiers started contributing chewing gum and whatever they had. They initially wrapped them in handkerchiefs. As word spread, however, American schools began sending candy attached to little parachutes—just pieces of cloth and strings. Halvorsen's crew would push the parachutes out the plane's back door. The small packages would fly all over because of the wind, dispersing over a fairly large area.

Other kids and I would run through the streets. Sometimes, you would see a whole lot of the parachutes, being blown this way and that way. Sometimes, they got stuck on the roofs of houses. I never got one. There was always too much competition. And, because the airport was so far away—and I still had to go to school—I was only able to go two or three times during the entire airlift. But I remember it distinctly, those little white things floating through the air. All of a sudden, they were dropping candy instead of bombs. To see this reversal, in a span of three years, was very emotional for us. That's when we, as kids, began to love the Americans.

Decades later, when I was Co-Chairman of the American Academy in Berlin, I was able to meet Gail Halvorsen and invite him to the Academy's Berlin villa, the cultural center that was created by the distinguished American diplomat Richard Holbrook when American troops finally left Berlin in 1994.

When I introduced Colonel Halvorsen at the villa, I explained to those in attendance that the blockade was a turning point in German-American relations because it turned enemies into friends. The "Candy Bomber" turned our appreciation for America into a love of America—that was the emotional part of it. The rest of it could be explained with geopolitical rationale and this and that. But this was a purely human-friendship gesture. It sort of ended the occupation; it was the beginning of peace for us.

With Gail Halvorsen in Berlin, 2011.

To me, the colonel deserves a lot of credit. He is a devout Mormon and very active in his church. He doesn't drink and doesn't smoke. In his own book, he writes about the fact that it was not necessarily easy to be a non-swearing, non-drinking, and non-smoking G.I. at that time. But apparently he was accepted, and his operation became a big success. It was truly one of the highlights of my life.

At that point—in late '48 and '49—we knew that we were going to make it in West Berlin. The Russians realized that the propaganda value of the airlift was enormous for the West. In May '49, the Russians finally caved in. They announced that the roads, rail links, rivers, and canals had been "repaired" and traffic could resume. The blockade ended. All this accelerated the popularity of the West and the unpopularity of the East to the Germans.

Afterward, until the Berlin Wall went up twelve years later, in 1961, if East Germans wanted to get out of East Germany they could go to East Berlin and then to West Berlin—although over time that would become more of a challenge.

SIX

WHEN FATHER RETURNED

This section relies partially on a report I wrote immediately after the event for my newspaper, Die Mücke.

We had no idea that my father was coming back until the day he arrived. It was on a Sunday in November of 1949, when I was thirteen, my brother was twenty, and my sister was seventeen. We had, at last, become the sole occupants of our house, and we—my mother, my brother, my sister, and I— were sitting in the living room, having, I believe, afternoon tea. My mother turned on the radio, and the announcer was reading off a list of names. It was customary that whenever German prisoners of war came back from Russia the local radio stations would call out their names.

The broadcasts weren't regularly scheduled; it was whenever the stations found out that a train, specially arranged, was arriving from the Soviet Union and they had been given the list. They would announce the names by district. We hardly ever bothered to listen, because it had been going on for years—POWs were returning all the time. But at that moment, since the announcer hadn't reached Spandau yet, someone said, "Well, we may as well listen." And that particular day, my father's name came up. We were completely shocked! Of course, we were elated.

Gisela remembers it a bit differently.

That is the sort of thing you never forget. The phone started ringing. The doorbell rang. And both of us, and Jürgen, we dashed in all directions. And people whom we had never seen before, but lived somewhere nearby, came over. The name Müller von der Heyden, many people knew the name. "You need to hear this. It was in the news . . ." or ". . . in a special report. Your father is coming home!" Then the next one arrived with the same news.

Uncle Hugo called too. He, of course, had heard the news as well. And he said to Mother, "Listen, this is how I . . . ." He already had a car at the time, which is worth mentioning. And he said, "I'll go to the Zoo Station with Jürgen and Ingolf tonight, not you two women. And Jürgen can put Ingolf on his shoulders. And we'll bring a photo of Father, and Ingolf can hold it in his hands because he will barely remember what his father looks like." And that's how you took off.

There were lots of practical issues that we had to deal with right away. For example, who would go to the train station to meet my father. That was not easy, because we had only three hours to get to the station that was somewhere in East Berlin. My mother decided not to go, so that she could get everything ready in the house. That was probably a smart move; we had no help in those days. My sister also stayed behind. So my brother and I went.

We had to take various means of public transportation to get to the station (Schlesischer Bahnhof—Silesia Station, now called "Ostbahnhof"), which was basically bombed-out, but was still in operation anyway, since the tracks were okay. When we arrived, the platform was packed with people like us who were waiting for family members. I remember climbing up on a lamppost in order to see. My brother, at six foot six, didn't have a problem.

At 9:43 p.m. the train—an old-fashioned train powered by a coal-fueled engine—arrived. It was pretty crowded. The doors opened and the prisoners of war poured out, hundreds of them. They were all dressed in a sort of gray-looking felt, Russian prisoner-of-war garb, and wearing fake fur hats. It was probably what Russian peasants wore.

It was nighttime and the light was poor, so it was difficult to find who we were looking for. But I think my brother and I spotted my father at just about the same time. At least I claim that. Of course, my brother claimed that he saw him first. In any case, we both saw him; he was thinner but still stood erect. We ran to him and embraced him. He didn't say much. He said, "You look well." "You look well, too," we replied. It was a little bit awkward because, after five years, we had gotten used to his being away. However, everything was temporarily overshadowed by the emotions of seeing each other again.

Of course there had been no way of communicating with our mother once we had left our house, but Uncle Hugo had said, "Bring your father to the Zoo Station" (in West Berlin close to his house). So the three of us took the elevated train there, where Uncle Hugo treated us to a beer. He didn't turn my father's return into a big deal. He said to him, "Glad you're back, wonderful to see you. Go home and see your wife." Then he drove us home but didn't come inside; he wanted to give us privacy. We had a joyful reunion.

In my conversation with Gisela, she said Jürgen had once described to her his version of what the reunion had been like.

At the station, Jürgen told me, women were standing on the stairs and holding up big photographs, asking, "Have you seen him? Do you know him? Have you heard from him?" And the pictures were of their sons and husbands.

It must have been pretty horrific. But you were able to spot Father and he must also have recognized you because Mother had occasionally been sending photos in the mail, the Feldpostkarten [authorized postcards].

Jürgen also told me that Uncle Hugo had said to Father, "We're not going home straightaway. First we're going to drink a Molle *[Berlin expression for a glass of beer] so that you know you're back home." We never used the word "Molle" at home. That really touched me. It was basically the first thing Father heard Uncle Hugo say.*

Once my father arrived home, he unpacked; he didn't have much, just one small satchel. Then he brought out a piece of bread, Russian bread. He and the other prisoners were pretty much on a starvation diet, but he had saved this bread for us; it was part of his rations. He thought that we needed it; he thought that West Germany was in terrible condition. In Russia, he had received only East German propaganda from the East German newspapers—if he received any German newspapers at all. And the papers were reporting that West Berliners were starving to death, while the workers' paradise of East Germany was thriving.

However at that point, we were pretty well off. The Russian bread, on the other hand, was awful. It was damp and *awful*. We laughed when we saw it and said, "That bread is shit; let's throw it away. We have better bread for you." We were all trying to impress him.

Of course, in retrospect, bringing that bread was actually an incredibly generous and loving act on my father's part. He was dumbfounded, just dumbfounded, at our reaction. I'm sure we hurt his feelings, because he would have expected us to be very grateful; he had saved his bread, and now it wasn't appreciated. I remember that, after that, he became very quiet.

Father returns home from a Soviet P.O.W. camp, November 1949.

Gisela also remembered our father's arrival at the house.

That's an image I will never forget. It was winter, everything was pretty bare in the garden and Father came up the long walkway, which curved a little toward the front door. He was shuffling his feet, but his posture was upright, and he was carrying this horribly dirty field bag over his shoulder. He was wearing these head warmers—ear warmers, a fur hat from Russia and just rags on his feet. That is how he arrived, in his old leather coat, encased in grime. I guess he had protected the coat like his own skin. Of course it was scuffed and everything, but it had protected him from the cold.

That is how he arrived. He didn't look like he had before. For me he was a stranger, a total stranger! He said, after he had hugged all of us, "I didn't come empty handed. I brought you something." He rummaged through the field bag and took out this horrible looking bread. He said, "This is what I brought you." He said, "They told us that you were starving here in Berlin." He was so disappointed that we . . . that there was no cheering. And then one of us, possibly me with my big mouth, said, "But we can feed it to our chickens tomorrow." In that moment his face turned to stone.

There was a little pause. He had the bread in his hands like this, and he looked at the bread and said, "Bread was gold to us." That's what he said. "Bread was gold to us." So we were embarrassed and Mother said, "But we've never had a bread like this, Werner. We are going to share it tomorrow for breakfast. And then everybody will have their piece . . . and we'll know what you ate in the . . ." That relaxed the situation.

Mother said, "You know what, Werner? I am sure you're looking forward to washing up. Let's go downstairs, not upstairs to the bathroom, but let's go downstairs to the laundry room."

As soon as she heard the news about Father, she had put the kettle on, the copper kettle, so there would be warm water downstairs when he arrived. And then someone, I don't know who it was, scooped the water into the tub and Father undressed down there. And Mother instantly shoved every-thing he had taken off, from the rags to the ear warmers, into the coal fire. Absolutely everything. She said, "They're all full of lice." And Father just looked at her with big eyes.

Mother told me later, "I had a chair standing there with his clothes laid out, all ready. But he just got a strange expression on his face and stared at his clothes that were . . . that had been his whole life for the last years, which were quickly disappearing in the flames. That took him quite a while to digest. It was as if we were from a different planet."[1]

I asked my sister what happened the next day.

Well, he asked us a lot of questions, especially in regards to school. And he told us how much we had grown and asked if we had any boyfriends/ girlfriends. And we answered all his questions, and then I said, "But now you have to tell us something about yourself." He said, "There isn't much to tell. We slept in barracks, thirty men per barrack, sometimes two per bed. And whatever valuables you had you needed to bury, hide well. Otherwise they would get stolen. Not only by the Russians, but also by the Germans."

That was about all he said at the beginning. Later, we heard that he had chopped wood. He said he needed to do something, and the work would get him an extra portion of soup at lunch. Most important, it kept him warm. The winters in the Urals were extremely cold and he had to dig graves every day. I know you mentioned Buchenwald. Maybe he also dug graves there, but he didn't talk about it. I remember he said, "We had to dig with a pickax because of the permafrost." That's what he told us. That was the first time I had heard the word "permafrost." I didn't know what that was.

After all that time, Father was like a foreign object among us. And he could feel that. He was always trying to slip back in, but then . . . He tried to turn back the clock, and wanted to continue raising us the way he had before he left. But that was no longer possible. We had a very good

---

[1] It is unlikely that the burning of the clothes took place that night because my father came home when it was dark; two photos exist of him in his Russian garments taken during daylight. It is likely that he put these garments back on the next day for the pictures and that they were then burned.

relationship with Mother, and she had developed a good diplomatic rapport with us over the years. But Father was very strict. He turned into a dictator, and he was also unpleasant and unsatisfied . . . which was understandable.

My memories are much the same. Within a day or so it became clear to Father that he had lost control of the family. He would try to tell Jürgen what to do, and my brother would just laugh. He had been taking care of things in my father's place. Now Father tried to reassert himself. I also think he probably still saw us as the kids we had been five years earlier. His whole mentality was different, old-fashioned. As democracy was taking hold in Germany, in *West* Germany, the autocratic rules of fathers-in-charge had disappeared because most of the men had been killed, and the women were basically running the country. He was not prepared for this totally new order. My mother was a superb manager. She actually had much better business skills than my father. I think my mother was never again as close to my father as she had been before the war. She had become independent, and he couldn't accept that.

After he was back, back in civilian clothes, he had to look for a job. He tried to gain a foothold again at Lufthansa in Bonn, though Gisela has said that Mother tried to talk him out of it. He was rejected. His former colleagues, who had not had the misfortune of being prisoners of war, had filled all of the available positions and considered him obsolete. Father was out of the picture. He knew that he couldn't knock on any more doors. That was the way it was.

But he was a metallurgist; he had received a diploma—like a Master's degree—in metallurgical engineering. So he got a job offer from a steel company in Oberhausen, in the middle of the Ruhr district—it's near Cologne, very densely populated, and there were smokestacks everywhere in those days.

He said to Mother, "I'm going to take this job, and I want you to come along." He may have been home about six months by then. My mother replied, "No." And he said, "Well, I'm going to go, and find housing, and then I'll come back and get you." He left, and later told her that he had found a place; he had rented a single room above a pub, in a very shabby part of Oberhausen. He said, "This is great, you know."

Luxury never meant anything to him. He thought the room was perfect. It was certainly a lot better than how he had lived the previous five years. He arranged for the whole family to join him, but Jürgen was already studying law at the Free University in Berlin and Gisela had taken the *Abitur*, the high school exit exams, and had left home; she was working for a chemical company in the Ruhr region as well, not far from Oberhausen.

My mother went to check it out and was horrified. She came back to Berlin and said, "We're not going to move."

According to Gisela, when Mother told him "You can't ask me to move— to leave this house," Father got extremely upset, and shouted, "We lost the war! We can't make any demands. This is where my job is. Over there, look over the factory walls, that's where the coal flows. And that is where I earn my money—and it is your duty to be there!"

Father stayed in Oberhausen by himself. Occasionally he saw Gisela, and occasionally he would visit, or my mother and I would visit him. That was the lowest point after Father's return.

The tensions between my mother and father escalated in other ways as well after the war. Gisela said that Mother told her, "Life with Father is no longer the way it used to be."

Nor could she sleep next to him anymore, because at night in his dreams he would relive the past. He would jump on her and shake her awake and say, "They didn't beat us! No, they didn't beat us!" He did that a few nights in a row. She said, "At first, I was terribly startled. And it would take me a long time to calm him down. I'd say, 'Werner, you're dreaming! You are back home now!' He would apologize but he kept having these nightmares." She said, "I can't sleep here with you anymore." That's how it really was.

During that time, he was involved in rebuilding a bridge across the Rhine, near Düsseldorf. (You always need metallurgists for heavy construction projects because the metals have to fit the occasion. The steel has to be right; the weight-bearing factors are critical.)

Standing on a bridge, under re-construction, across the Rhine near Düsseldorf.

On one of our visits, I saw the bridge before it was finished. They were constructing it from both sides and there was a gap in the middle. My father allowed me—I was fifteen years old then—to go onto the bridge, which was high above the Rhine, and walk toward the center as far as the bridge had been completed. At the end there was a bush or tree stuck into the grating. I remember looking down into the abyss.

In response to me looking down, he said, "Well, let me take you below." Down below there were a number of foundations, maybe four feet by four feet. Each foundation was made up of two cones: one that came to a point, like an ice cream cone, which was not more than ten inches in diameter; and one that sat atop it, upside down. The whole bridge rested on these balancing cones. My father was right in his element; he understood exactly how it worked. For the first time, I saw the value of his education and his profession, and was very proud of him. Even so, after my father returned, he was never able to support us financially in any tangible way.

I had always had a good relationship with him, and, when he returned from Russia, I thought we would become closer than the way it turned out to be. He was always gone. And when he was around, he was moody and often autocratic. So we had our arguments. But, yes, I loved him. I loved my father.

When he was still a prisoner of war, I would occasionally play a game at school with my friends, whose fathers were also Russian prisoners of war. We would dare one another: What would you do if it could make your father come back tomorrow? Would you sacrifice a finger of your hand? Which finger? Or would you sacrifice a whole hand? It would turn into one-upmanship as to what we would sacrifice if we could get our fathers back.

When they came home, many of them suffered from post-traumatic stress. I don't know if my father actually had PTSD, but, according to my mother, he was a very different man. Before the war, he had been a fun-loving guy, an athlete, and a great skier. They had taken trips to Italy, and gone kayaking and boating around Berlin. They had also had lots of friends and parties and so on. His gregariousness never came back.

Except for the few questions he answered on his return, he never talked about his five years in Russia. Never. We, my siblings and I, respected that. We didn't ask a lot of questions. So it was mutual. But now I wish that I had, and that he had talked about it. The most he told us was that he had been in various camps—which we already knew. And occasionally he would say, "Well, in camp we did such and such." Very matter of fact. Over time, we learned that there were probably hundreds of prisoners in each camp, and there seemed to have been a very strong camaraderie among the German prisoners of war. They were apparently largely self-governing; the Russians left them alone. I don't believe he was concerned about being killed. He was an officer, and the Russians respected the Geneva Convention. Nevertheless, he lived under very difficult conditions.

Toward the end of his life, Gisela observed just how emotionally distant he had become.

Father would sit outside in the evenings, most often at sunset; he would take Grandmother's old wicker chair out of the garden shed and sit by the poplar trees and look out onto the Havel River. And Mother would say, "He's been sitting there already for two hours now, barely moving." His life was probably passing through him over and over again . . .

SEVEN

PEACETIME

Gradually, after the Berlin Blockade was over and after my father came back, the (West) German "economic miracle" took hold. People became more prosperous. VW brought out the "Bug," and people started buying cars again. It all seemed fairly normal.

However, what wasn't normal was that our daily companion was now the Cold War. Our disgust with the Soviet regime, and in particular, with the proxy Communist German regime that the Soviets had set up, became more intense. The people in the East began to realize that they lived under a puppet regime controlled by the Soviets, and that, by contrast, West Germany was able to hold free elections. Ironically, East Germany still had several political parties. But that didn't mean anything; they all voted the same way.

The next big political event occurred on June 17, 1953.

At that point, I was in high school, the *Gymnasium*, and coincidentally, on that day we had a so-called school expedition: a field trip that took us into the northern part of Berlin, into some wooded area, near one of the border crossings between West Berlin and East Germany. It was right in the middle of the woods—as a matter of fact, most roads that went from West Berlin to East Germany (as opposed to East Berlin) were sort of in the middle of the woods.

The border crossing was basically a red-and-white barrier to stop traffic— like a gate in a parking lot—that was operated manually (you could lift the barrier with one hand) by a cop, who would check your papers. If you were a West Berliner, you couldn't simply enter East Germany without going through the right steps.

Anyway, when we arrived at the crossing, the barrier was in the upright position. There was nobody there, which was unheard of—quite sensational. That just didn't happen. We immediately knew that something was wrong. We finally found out that there was a workers' demonstration going on in East Berlin; it had started in the factories. The students and the intelligentsia were yet to be involved. The fact that the factory workers were causing the unrest made the situation even worse for the Communists. Those were the very people whom the government was supposedly taking care of. That was pretty much the end of the field trip because several of us said, "We have to go there."

So we made our way by public transportation to the West Berlin–East Berlin line, which was still wide open. By the time we got to the center of the city, it was very exciting. People, by the hundreds, by the *thousands*, were milling around. Before we arrived, the factory workers had been throwing rocks—Belgian blocks pried from the sidewalks—at the Russian tanks. The tanks had already left the scene.

Prior to that day, the Russian heavy military equipment had largely remained out of sight. There were half a million Russian soldiers stationed around Berlin. By comparison, there were perhaps 10,000 American and fewer British and French troops stationed in West Berlin. But the East Germans hadn't really fully remilitarized. So when the demonstrations started, the East Germans had to call the Russians for help. All of a sudden, in the middle of Berlin, the Russian tanks had reappeared.

I saw a lot of broken windows. I saw paper all over the place, because apparently some of the workers had raided and vandalized certain Communist offices, throwing the files out of the windows. There was a general commotion, but there was no enemy that the workers could get hold of. The East Berlin regime was pretty well protected.

The authorities started arresting the leaders of the uprising. Of course, they had the Stasi, their secret police, who were all over the place, among the crowds, identifying myriad people. They made numerous arrests in the following days.

The unrest lasted just a day. Then it was over. It was similar to the Hungarian uprising in 1956, and the Czech revolution in Prague, some fifteen years later. Those were also put down by Russian tanks. The problem in '53 was that there were calls for democracy, but nobody showed up. The East German politicians hid themselves away.

I should point out that the violent clashes did not happen only in Berlin; they took place all over East Germany, and in some parts they were actually more brutal. For me it was very interesting, because it was the first time that it became clear that the East Germans were willing to fight for their freedom and for democracy. It became even clearer that the puppet Russian regime in East Germany didn't represent the people, in any way, shape, or form.

I was initially very disappointed that the uprising had been crushed. It could have been a seminal event, because it was the first real revolt in Germany against an existing government. Germans have always been accused—and maybe rightly so—of being good underlings, good citizens, under whatever government they had. The difference between the Hitler regime and the Soviet-imposed regime was that most Germans actually supported the Hitler regime. This was a voluntary thing. But most people did not support the East German regime. (It's a miracle to me that it survived for another thirty-five or thirty-six years until 1989.)

In the 1950s, little by little, there were more and more restrictions in East Germany. And, with two currencies in place, when East Berliners came to West Berlin, they had to first exchange their Marks at the free-market rate: four-to-one, or five-to-one, and the imbalance got progressively worse. They couldn't afford anything in West Berlin, and it became harder and harder for them to work there.

Still there were no official travel restrictions between the two halves until the wall went up in 1961. The subways ran all around the city. All the same, like in any big city, most East Berliners tended to stay in their own districts and their own neighborhoods, instead of traveling back and forth between East and West—except, perhaps, those who lived near the line. As for the East Germans from other areas, they also had to have documents to enter East Berlin; but that was difficult to enforce because there were daily commuter trains coming in from the countryside.

My daily life finally seemed fairly ordinary. I continued to go to soccer games. However, the West Berlin teams only played in West Berlin. I was going to high school in Spandau and would bike there as well; it was about a half-hour bike ride, each way.

In those days, there were thirteen years of required schooling in order to go to university. I was not what you would call a diligent student. In the early years, when I was ten, eleven, or twelve, even though I was already at the Gymnasium, everything came to me easily. I didn't study much but got good grades anyway.

But, in math, as you know, everything builds on what you've previously learned. If you don't have the fundamentals right, you cannot really advance. I was fuzzy about the fundamentals and, later on, I was lost in math class. Of course, I didn't want to admit it, and I had trouble passing the math exams. The mathematics that you learn at the German Gymnasium takes you all the way through calculus. So I had trouble with that and my math grades were average, at best, but I did pass.

I excelled in both history and German. I was also good in Greek. We had seven years of Greek and nine years of Latin. We started at age ten with Latin. At age twelve, our second foreign language was Greek—seven years of it because we graduated at nineteen. English came when we were fifteen, as the third (fourth, if you count German) language. My school was called a "classical" Gymnasium, where they stressed the ancient languages; it was also called a "humanistic" Gymnasium. Aside from the classical Gymnasium, you could instead attend a science-oriented Gymnasium, and there was also a modern-language one. Basically the model for the classical approach came from Wilhelm von Humboldt in the nineteenth century. The initial idea was that an educated German should be able to read the Bible in the original languages. The Bible consists mainly of four languages: Hebrew, Aramaic, Greek, and Latin; and so Germans had to learn those four languages in order to read the entire Bible in the original.

Hebrew was later abandoned—but not due to Hitler. Hebrew had been stopped in the early twentieth century, as was Aramaic. The impetus to learn all four foreign languages faded as the country became more secular. Latin and Greek, however, were—and are—considered the foundation stones of Western civilization. In Latin, we read Caesar, Tacitus, and the like. In Greek, we read Homer, *The Odyssey* and *The Iliad*; we read history by Herodotus and Thucydides; we read Plato and the great Greek playwrights.

I loved Greek. But I disliked Latin; I had trouble with it. I don't know why. I thought Greek was a much more melodic language, and it had a huge and incredibly rich vocabulary.

The Odyssey and *The Iliad* have hundreds of words that show up nowhere else in Greek literature. There is no possible way you can memorize them all. I would constantly sit with the dictionary, looking up words, but there was no point in trying to memorize them. The poems came from as many as eight hundred years before Christ, whereas the prime of the Greek culture was some five hundred years before Christ. So, by the height of Greek culture, it was already a different language. And of course, modern Greek is even more different.

The German educational system was very rigorous; they separated kids at age ten according to their potential. You either went to the Gymnasium, with a small percentage of students, or you went to a preparatory school called a *Realschule*, or practical school, through tenth grade. If you went to a Realschule, you would not qualify for a university education. But there were ways to transfer back and forth in the interim. If you were particularly talented in the Realschule—or you were a real loser in the Gymnasium—you could switch.

Today's German education has been watered down. It's no longer as elitist as it was. Each federal state has different standards. For instance, Bavaria in the south has the highest standards. They still have some Gymnasiums that are like the one I went to. But, in Berlin, in the big cities, where the Social Democrats have won, they have leveled the playing field. I'm not saying that's good or bad; I'm just saying that's what happened.

Anyway, I had a great awakening at age seventeen. I realized that I couldn't fake the math anymore and needed to buckle down. The exit exam, the *Abitur*, was a five-hour written test in the main subjects; and, a few months after that, there were oral exams, which covered the whole nine years. So it became scarier and scarier to think about these tests; it kept me up at night. I finally realized that I had to do something, because if you got two F's in any two subjects at the end of the school year you had to repeat the whole year—even the courses you had passed.

The other students and I had always been together as a class. While the teachers changed depending on the subject, we took every subject together. We started with forty-eight students in our class (there could be several classes in the same grade)—and forty-eight was more or less the maximum per class. But the school administrators knew that the number would shrink. Kids would either drop out or have to stay back a year. We also had those who had stayed back from the year before.

In the end, I actually got a decent grade in math. I received good grades in Greek, German, and history, and pretty decent grades in music, biology, chemistry, and physical education. When I graduated in 1955, out of the original forty-eight, sixteen of us finished with the *Abitur*.

Except for a few subjects, I hated high school. The relentless pressure to do homework and get good grades got to me. I had no self-discipline. Some of the teachers had been Nazis, and they still lorded it over us. I loathed them. They would say: "Later in life, you will look back to your time here and declare it the happiest years in your life!" I didn't believe it then—and I haven't changed my mind since.

Long before my graduation, life in our household had settled down. My father had kept trying to get a job back in Berlin. Finally, after about a year, he found a job with a company and settled into a routine. The company he worked for developed an audio tape-recording machine. It was actually a very good product. The tape, which was one of the first of its kind, was in a cassette—like a videotape, but it was wider. It was unique and revolutionary, but the company that made it didn't have enough capital and eventually went bankrupt.

My father read the newspaper every day, listened to the radio, and became interested in West German politics. In 1950, there was an election coming up. In Germany, you vote for the party, not for a person. There were basically three parties: the Christian Democrats, the Social Democrats, and the Free Democrats. I asked my father for whom he would vote. He said, "I am going to vote for the Free Democrats." I asked, "Why?" And he said, "Because of Ludwig Erhard." Erhard was the most admired man in Germany, and he was a likeable guy. The problem was that Ludwig Erhard was a candidate for the Christian Democrats, not the Free Democrats. When it came to politics, my father was still clueless. "You know that Ludwig Erhard is a Christian Democrat," I told him. He said, "Oh, really? That can't be right. I have been following this." I realized that he didn't even know that the party he was going to vote for wasn't the party of his favorite guy.

Meanwhile my mother also had developed her own routine. And I had my routine. We all got along pretty well, although ours was not what you would call a really close family. We were all very independent of one another.

My brother lived at home while he was working toward his law degree at the Free University in Berlin, where he had been one of the founding students. The university was created as the answer when Berlin's university, the Humboldt University, ended up on the Communist side in East Berlin. Having no university was unacceptable, and so a group of professors and students created the Free University. It was called "Free" not because there was no tuition, but because it was located in "Free Berlin." (Almost everything in West Berlin was called "free.")

We learned that the schools and the textbooks in the GDR were filled with propaganda—just like they had been under the Nazis. We would hear about the curricula. The East Germans were good in math, engineering, and the sciences, which cannot be politicized. In the arts, including history, they were awful. You saw the same distortions that the Nazis did to history—except now you saw it from the Communist perspective.

I would go over to East Berlin sometimes and buy newspapers and books just to see how things were being discussed. Like the textbooks, popular non-fiction books were filled with propaganda; they essentially said that the East Germans were victims of fascism. They tried to turn themselves into victims.

The regime's ability to control the media, however, was spotty. East Berlin had no independent newspapers; for a while, I think, you could buy West Berlin newspapers in East Berlin, but that was stopped by the authorities fairly soon after the war. Later on, the authorities seized anybody with a Western newspaper, making it unpleasant for those who got caught. In spite of that, everybody listened to the radio, to Western radio stations. And, as soon as television became available, the East Berliners could watch Western television. However, the West Berlin stations could only reach so far inside East Germany. If you lived in Dresden or Leipzig, you couldn't get Western television. Movie theaters in East Berlin were a different matter; most films made in the West would not be shown. The officials tried to isolate East Germany as much as possible. (That was even more pronounced in Poland and in other Soviet Bloc countries.)

I would spend time with a close group of friends. We found time to write plays and stories, and even record them. Because of my father's work, I was able to get hold of one of the tape recorders. We loved it. We recorded detective stories and everything.

When my friends and I were fifteen, we would get together to have an occasional beer at a nearby local bar. There was no such thing as carding someone; I don't even know whether there was an official drinking age. Drinking and driving was never an issue. None of us drove. Nobody had a car, and even if someone's parents had a car, they sure as hell didn't let their kid drive it. It was too precious. My own parents didn't have a car until later.

I continued to work on my newspaper, *Die Mücke*, and on the school's, *Hornisse*, to which I contributed articles about theater, as I loved to go to both the theater and the opera. I saw *Die Hornisse* as just a larger version of *Die Mücke*. I started to fill *Die Mücke* with stories I wrote about my experiences, and about things in general. Gisela liked to write poetry, so I also published her poems.

In the summers, I took bicycle trips all over Germany and even up to Denmark and Sweden. It was all very adventurous, and I wrote articles about those trips as well. My first trip was when I was fifteen; I bicycled alone through West Germany. Before leaving, I wasn't sure whether I would get my parents' permission. I prepared myself for defending the trip and telling them why I would be safe. When I told them that I wanted to go, they said, "Fine, great." No ifs, no buts, not a single question, just "Go and do it." And that was that.

As I've said, in order to get from West Berlin to West Germany, you had to travel through East Germany. But, since West Berliners were not allowed to bike through East Germany, people on bicycles had to ask truckers for rides at the checkpoints into East Germany. It never took very long to get a ride, in my experience, and the truckers were incredibly helpful. I don't think I was ever charged any money.

I mostly bicycled by myself but sometimes teamed up with someone else. When we got to the hilly and mountainous country in the south of Germany, we would wait for a slow-moving truck and then hang on to the back of it and get a free ride up the hill—which was a huge help since my bike had only one gear. The truck drivers hated it but there wasn't much they could do about it. Sometimes, I even bicycled at night.

One time, I wrote a story about Uncle Hugo (who was still contributing letters to the editor), who gave me money for a bicycle light. I went to buy it the next day, and it turned out he had given me the exact amount of the purchase. He had known down to the last penny how much it cost.

I also published a daily diary. At night, we stayed at youth hostels, which were incredibly cheap. We could get a hot soup for about forty Pfennig (twenty cents). En route, we helped ourselves to the ripe fruit growing near the road on farms and gardens and filled our canteens with milk from containers the farmers had put out on the road for pickup by the dairies.

Everybody said, "Well, his obsession with his newspapers is one of those phases he's going through." But, for me, it was a way to make some money, since my parents couldn't afford to give me any. And, over time, *Die Mücke* turned out to be lucrative.

My family lived pretty frugally because my father's job didn't really pay that much, and my mother had stopped working at my father's insistence. We had gained full control of the main house again; but my parents rented out the smaller wing of the main house, where my grandmother had once lived, as well as the little house on the property, to supplement our income. The times were tight, economically, throughout the '50s.

EIGHT

AN UNEXPECTED DEVELOPMENT

I wanted to become a journalist in the worst way. When I told Uncle Hugo that I wanted to study journalism after I graduated from high school, he very cleverly talked me out of it. He said, "That's a great idea. Journalism is a great profession." He advised me, however, not to become a generalist (the sort of reporter who writes about current events), but to become a specialist—one who reports on a specific field, such as sports or business. He suggested that I become a business journalist. He said that what I should do is study business first, become an expert, and then write about it. That way I could make more money, and it would be more prestigious. That made sense to me. So we talked about business management training programs, and Uncle Hugo recommended one with a bank. That's how he succeeded in sneaking me into the business world, where he wanted me to be all along.

It is fairly common in Germany to take a break from your academic studies between high school and university to learn a craft or profession as a trainee. There was a philosophy in Germany—which I think is not a bad philosophy—that between high school and college, kids should get some practical experience. Rigorous training programs, supported by industry and the government, still exist in almost every field; they are the now well-known German apprentice system.

With Uncle Hugo's help, I entered a banking program with Berliner Bank AG in Berlin. I worked five full days a week, and half days on Saturdays, in the bank; on two of those days, I attended an apprentice school in the morning, where we were taught accounting, commercial law, and other topics that would have been difficult to pick up on the job. I earned sixty Deutsche marks a month—about fifteen dollars at the exchange rate then. It was not enough to live on, but apprentices' parents were still expected to take care of them.

The idea of the training was to expose you to every job at the bank, from the bottom up. So I started in the mailroom, stuffing bank statements into envelopes, etc. There were no computers in those days. Every time a customer or a business had any activity in their accounts, a machine printed out a new account statement, which was then addressed using a metal address plate. These address plates were in long trays. I would put the appropriate address plate and account statement in the addressing machine, stamp the address on the statement, and then mail the statement. That was my job: find the metal plate; stamp the statement; mail it out. (Later, in America, when I was working for Pitney-Bowes, they bought the company—Adrema Werke—that made these plates. I was sent back to Berlin for two months to install a standard-cost accounting system. When computers eventually made addressing plates obsolete, Adrema Werke went under.)

After the mailroom, I became a collector of IOU notes. As Germany recovered from the war, most people didn't have bank credit, and there were no credit cards. In order to buy furniture or other big-ticket items, people would go to a bank and sign bills of exchange, or "promissory notes." If, for example, they needed to borrow a thousand marks, they would get ten promissory notes—a hundred marks each, payable once a month. The preferred practice in those days was for the customer to come to the bank whenever a note was due and bring the money. That would have been great, but most people didn't do it. So I—as one of the apprentices—had to go to their homes, ring the bell, present the bill, and try to collect.

The particular branch to which I was assigned, Branch #41, was at the corner of Tauentzienstrasse and Nürnberger Strasse, right in the middle of the red light district. We always had to guess when these people would be at home. I knew that the hookers would likely be there early in the day because they mostly worked at night. So I would show up at 8:00 or 8:30 a.m. and ring the bell, sometimes five or six times. Initially, I wasn't really sure whether it would be a hooker's apartment—I had been told that sometimes the prostitutes would give the bank someone else's address. But if a hooker was there, she would typically come to the door with her bathrobe half open, sleepy eyes, and mascara running down her face, looking awful. I would say, "Hello, I'm from Berliner Bank. I want to present this promissory note for payment." And she would sigh, and—occasionally—she would reach into her bra and pull out some dirty-looking money. I have to say, those experiences cured me of ever hiring a prostitute right there and then!

Except, there was one advantage in my meeting the 'ladies of the evening.' I had a motor scooter, which I rode to work. I also used it to go to the opera and the theater, and I would sometimes park it under the bridge that was part of Zoo Station, which was close to most of the theaters. You can't really secure scooters too well, but some hookers would hang out under the bridge—particularly when it rained. I would say hi to them, and maybe "good to see you," and sometimes they would offer to keep an eye on my scooter. They all had a great sense of humor, even though I never patronized any of them. I don't think they expected me to—they knew I had no money.

Occasionally, when the bank branch I worked at was short of cash, another trainee and I would have to walk to the main office of the bank, which was maybe a ten-minute walk away in the heart of West Berlin's commercial district. We would pick up hundreds of thousands of marks (in excess of $100,000) in bills—an enormous amount for most citizens—and stash them into an ordinary briefcase. Then we would walk as nonchalantly as we could through the crowded Zoo district back to our branch. The bank managers told us that it was the safest way to transport money on short trips—because nobody would expect a couple of youngsters to carry that much money. But there always had to be two of us.

Working in the mailroom, collecting from the prostitutes, and transporting cash were only the beginning of the training program. Over the two years, I learned every aspect of commercial banking. I worked in the credit department, the mortgage department, the cashier's department, and in the administrative division. At the end, I had to take an exam; I passed it and received a title: bank merchant, *Bankkaufmann*. (To Germans, titles are very important.)

During the two-year program, as I suspect Uncle Hugo had privately predicted, I began to find business appealing and dropped the idea of a career in journalism for good. As my apprenticeship was coming to an end, however, I began thinking about university. It was then that the possibility of coming to the United States to attend Duke University unexpectedly arose.

In 1956, my brother, then a full-time lawyer, had gone to New York City for a year because many of his clients were there. He had gotten married just before leaving for America, and he and his wife celebrated their honeymoon with a trip by boat over to America.

In the spring of 1957, Dr. Hans Lowenbach, a prominent psychiatrist and professor of psychiatry at Duke University, invited them to North Carolina to spend the Easter holiday with him and his family in Durham. He was a German secular Jew who had been a friend of my sister-in-law's family in Germany. When Jürgen and his wife, Erika (another Erika!), saw Duke's beautiful campus, my brother said, "I have a younger brother who could really benefit from improving his English." Jürgen, recognizing that the world was becoming more global and that languages were extremely important, asked, "Do you think he could study somewhere in America for a year?" Dr. Lowenbach said that it was certainly a possibility; he said that I would have to apply, and asked Jürgen about my credentials. Dr. Lowenbach was familiar with the German educational system, so when Jürgen told him about my background, he said, "Oh, no problem." He thought that I could get into any college in America and that I should apply to Duke; he would put in a good word for me.

I personally had never thought much about going to America, although many Germans fancied going to the US, Canada, or Australia. Aside from the US, Canada was popular with Germans, simply because—for some of them—it wasn't the US, and it had equally wide-open spaces. They said it had a more "European" culture. Australia, on the other hand, was considered enticing because it was an exotic, faraway land.

My brother sent me a letter, saying he had done some research. He wrote, "Here are some universities that I think you should apply to. Write a letter, explain everything." I think he had listed Harvard, Yale, Princeton—all the predictable candidates. The University of Michigan was also on the list, as well as a couple of outliers. And Duke.

I had never heard of Duke University, but I began to get excited. It was only expected to be for one year, and my parents were okay with that. We were all used to the system in Germany, where you can apply to university, attend a couple of semesters, and drop out or go to another university. I didn't know about freshman year, sophomore, and all that, or about the rigorous college curriculum. I just thought I would go over, take some English courses—all language-oriented—maybe learn a little bit about American government, and stuff like that.

At that time, I was occasionally dating a girl from Philadelphia—Sandy Calloway, an exchange student in Berlin on a program sponsored by the American Friends Service Committee, a Quaker organization. (Sandy was cute as a button, and remarkably, she had flown a small plane cross-country when she was fourteen years old—the first cross-country trip piloted by a fourteen-year-old girl.). I don't remember how I met her. I asked her to help me put my applications—just letters really—into proper English before I sent them off. The result was that I got accepted at two or three universities. But financial aid was essential, and none of them would give me a scholarship sight unseen—except for Duke, because of Dr. Lowenbach.

I had to apply for a student visa, which required a medical exam; I flunked it initially. For some reason, they spotted something on my lungs that would have prevented the whole thing. Dr. Unholtz, who was the father of my more serious girlfriend, Linde, said, "Let's take another picture." He concluded that I had "galloping pneumonia," which wasn't a problem, and he gave me a clean bill of health. So there I was, at age twenty-one, ready to conquer America—at least that's what I thought.

PART II
AMERICA

ONE

GO WEST

The passenger liner, the *Italia*, left from the North Sea port city of Bremerhaven. A ticket to America cost $200 for a place in a six-man bunk room, deep in the hold of the ship. My parents couldn't afford it—after all, $200 was a lot of money. But, with the money I had earned at the bank, I was able to purchase the ticket myself.

Off to America on the MS *Italia*, 1957.

We set sail in August of 1957, just after I had turned twenty-one. The voyage took eleven days because we made two stops: first in Cherbourg, France, and then in Southampton, England. For me, it was a truly great experience.

There were dozens of young people on board, and we partied every night. Right before we arrived in New York, we danced until dawn because we would be docking in New York at 7 a.m. Close to sunrise, everyone stood at the railing to see who would be the first to spot America. It was still pitch dark, but we could see car lights—I learned later that they were from somewhere on Long Island, perhaps people going to work. The boat began going more slowly; it entered New York Harbor and passed by the Statue of Liberty. Gliding up the Hudson to the Thirty-fourth Street pier, we were glued to the Manhattan side of the ship. It was overwhelming; my adrenaline was pumping. It seemed as if everything was about to happen.

We all disembarked, went through immigration, and had to find our luggage. On the pier, the crew had lined up the luggage for the whole ship, arranged according to the first letter of your family name, which created an immediate problem for me. My actual name back then was Ingolf Müller–von der Heyden. My father's last name was Müller—my mother's was von der Heyden. In the '20s, since Müller was the most common name in Germany, the German government (and also Lufthansa, where my father worked) encouraged people whose name was Müller to combine that name with their spouse's name. So my father, Werner Müller, became Werner Müller–von der Heyden. My mother, Erika von der Heyden, became Erika Müller–von der Heyden. And my given name was Ingolf, my first name. Not Karl. (That change came later.) So there on the pier it took me a while to find my luggage, because nobody knew where my last name started—with the letter M, or V, or H. It quickly became clear that my name was too complicated for America. Decades earlier, at Ellis Island, some immigration official probably would have simplified my name for me.

I had already bought my bus ticket from New York to Durham, NC, on board the ship from the agent Greyhound had stationed there. So, after I located my bag, I took it to the Port Authority Bus Terminal, and checked it, since my bus wasn't to leave until that evening. The first thing I did after that was to head to the Empire State Building . . . and to ride up the elevator. When I stepped out I could see that it was hazy—but there was still a pretty good view of the skyline and Manhattan. There were two very American-looking old ladies. They seemed old to me at the time, at least, and though now I realize that they had to have been tourists, in those days, I had no idea. They had a blue rinse on their graying hair that was common back then. As I was standing there, they asked, "Pardon me, is that the United Nations?" And they pointed to the Chrysler Building. I recognized the buildings from pictures I had seen; I said, "No," and pointed to the correct building. They looked at me, and said, "Oh, thank you very much." They probably thought they were talking to a native New Yorker! And I had been in the country for only two hours. I thought, "Boy, in two hours, I'm already giving directions. This is my city, this is great!" I loved it immediately.

My next stop was lunch. I went into a modest restaurant, where I ordered some food, and when the check came I didn't know what to do about the tip. In Germany, there would be a service charge included, and then you gave a modest additional tip. You usually handed the money to the waiter or waitress. So I put together some money, which I later realized probably was totally inadequate as a tip. I wanted to give it to the waitress, but she was running around. She had already left the change from my bill on my table, so she wouldn't be coming back to me. I didn't know what to do. Finally, I caught her eye and said, "I have a tip," and she said, "Just leave it on the table." I'm sure it was clear to her that she was dealing with a really ignorant foreigner, and she didn't have any time to waste on me.

I don't remember what I actually did for the rest of the afternoon. I didn't go to any museums; I think I just wandered around since after lunch I didn't have all that much time.

The bus to North Carolina may have left around six or seven o'clock—sometime in the early evening. Almost the minute I sat down I fell asleep; the overnight trip took something like twelve hours. The bus seemed fine, but I had nothing to compare it to; I had never ridden long-distance buses in Germany. When I woke up, it was early morning; although I don't know for sure, we were probably already in North Carolina. In 1957, there were no interstates; as I looked outside, we were on a two-lane highway. There were farms left and right. I saw my first cotton fields—with their little white cotton clumps—and acres of tobacco. And I saw shacks with black people. A lot of the fields, I found out, were tenant farms. I instantly realized that I was in a totally different world, a world that I could never have imagined.

When I arrived at Duke University, the campus seemed like a Gothic wonderland. It was quite beautiful, but I felt it was phony because it was built in the twentieth century. I asked myself why anyone with any sense of time and architecture—and history—would try to copy Gothic architecture in the twentieth century. The campus was then only twenty-nine years old. Nobody in Europe would have dreamed of putting up a Gothic building in that day and age.

I stepped off the bus with my one suitcase. I thought I was going to suffocate. It was like stepping into a steam bath—and I probably was wearing a coat and tie. I had never experienced humidity like that—instantly my shirt, pants—*everything*—clung to my body, and I was really, really uncomfortable. Nevertheless, I had to find the Allen Building, the administration building, to report to the Dean of Students.

When I arrived, the dean said, "Where have you been? We are four days into freshman orientation week." And I said, "What is freshman orientation week?" I had no idea about anything having to do with American universities—zero. They had sent a letter stating the date that I should arrive, but I hadn't taken it seriously. After all, in Germany, the high schools are very tightly organized but the universities are *laissez-faire*—in the name of academic freedom. For example, if a lecture started at three o'clock, the manual would say "15:00 p.t.", which meant "*pro tempora.*" In other words, there was an allowance of about fifteen minutes; so the professor usually wouldn't show up until 3:15. I should also add that the German view was that, when you enter university, you're basically a mature person, and you should be able to pursue your studies without a lot of supervision. Had I been going to a university in Germany, it would have been assumed that I was a serious research-oriented person who went to lectures and produced results without the need of strict time management. When that is the rule, you don't need the kind of babysitting that you get in German high schools—or in American colleges.

The dean noticed my befuddlement but simply said, "By the way, there is a mathematics placement test that starts in fifteen minutes. You need to go over there and take that test." He took my suitcase, pointed out the physics building, and told me to come back after I had finished. It was quite a walk and I made it there just in time. I was handed a pencil and a little blue book and told to sit at one of the small desks. Everyone in the room was already feverishly working on solving the problems. Then I realized the exam was in English—of course! It started with the simple stuff. But the simple stuff turned out to be insurmountable for me, because the questions were: "What if this is six inches and this is nine inches, etc.? What is the distance?" But I had never heard of an inch. I had never heard of a foot. I had never heard of an ounce. I had no concept of the measurement system being used. I couldn't answer any of the questions. When I reached the abstract math I was more comfortable; I was certain I had flunked all the early parts but probably passed the later, more difficult ones.

When I went back to the dean's office, I told the dean that I didn't know about feet and so on. He said, well, "We'll review this, and we'll take care of it." I also told him that I wanted to shorten my name to Ingolf Mueller—"ue" being the equivalent to the umlaut (¨) on the "u."

Then he asked me how much money I had on me. I said, "Twenty dollars," which was true.

He said, "What?"

"Twenty dollars, because I have a scholarship."

And he said, "But that's just for tuition. You know what tuition is?"

"No, I don't know what tuition is."

"That's just the fee, the student fee."

In those days, the tuition was a couple thousand dollars, which was the amount of my scholarship. To me, that was a fortune. I thought that would cover everything. I thought that for two thousand dollars I could live like a prince because the German university fees were very low—like fifty dollars a year—since the government subsidized everything.

He said, "No . . . It doesn't cover your books, it doesn't cover your room. It doesn't cover your food." And he sat there, getting paler and paler. And then he said, "Well, we have to do something about it, don't we? I will see what kind of part-time jobs we can find for you, because you'll have to earn some money here."

He directed me to the building where my room was located, in Building P. It was hotter than hell; it wasn't air-conditioned (I believe that many buildings at Duke still aren't today). There was a student advisor, an upperclassman who was very nice and wore an armband and looked very official. My room was P-108, on the ground floor. I started unpacking.

I unpacked the stuff my mother had put together for me, including a really good bottle of German white wine for Dr. Lowenbach as a thank-you gift. I set the wine on the chest of drawers, and the student advisor almost had a heart attack. In those days, Duke was a Methodist school, more or less. He said, "Alcohol is illegal on campus." First, I didn't understand—the very concept that there could be a problem with wine was hard to fathom. I said, "It's a gift for Dr. Lowenbach." The fellow said that he didn't care and that I was really in trouble. He said, "I have to report you—you know, under the honor code. And that means an automatic expulsion."

This whole thing went right by me. I said, "What? What? What are you talking about?"

He said, "Oh, I . . . I don't know—I can't *not* report you, but I know that you don't know. Let me see what I can do."

Thankfully, my student advisor was able to straighten the situation out. The following weekend, when Dr. Lowenbach invited me to his house, I gave him the bottle and told him the story. He laughed and said, "Yeah, that's the way it is here, in the South. Nothing we can do about it."

My first day was quite the day. It hadn't been easy, and I was pretty agitated. There was also the language problem. For the first time, I was hearing Southern accents, which were difficult to understand. Then my roommate showed up.

I had no idea that I was to get a roommate. I thought my two thousand-dollar scholarship would probably give me a nice apartment, and I would show up for some lectures for a year, have a good time, travel around America, and go back home.

Luckily, as it turned out my roommate was to be Jim Whitlock, who later joined the State Department. Jim had requested a German roommate in order to learn German; he already had taught himself Spanish. He had been under-educated in a little school in Maxton, North Carolina, but he was very smart and personable. He wanted to learn German, and I was the only German student at Duke University.

Jim was a real character. We got along brilliantly—our only arguments were about keeping the window open or closed in the winter; I liked to have the windows open, and Jim, a Southerner, wanted to have them closed. We had that constant battle, back and forth, but became great friends nevertheless.

My most pressing problem at the start of the school year was to get a part-time job, or several. With the dean's help, the school came back to me with some possibilities. The first thing they offered was for me to entertain kids in some kind of day care center, and read books to them. It was hopeless though—my English wasn't good enough. It was a remarkably bad idea. Finally, after a couple of other things that didn't work out, they said, "We have a really good solution for you. You can work in the cafeteria in the hospital. And your job will be . . . there are various jobs."

The first job I had was to take the food trays from the hospital people after they had eaten—not the patients, but the physicians, nurses, and student nurses; they brought me their trays and I would put them in a dumbwaiter on the way to the kitchen. Sometimes they would pile up because there were too many, and then I had to rearrange them. (That was the "skilled" part of the job.) Occasionally, I would have to go downstairs and work in the kitchen on the receiving end—unloading the trays from the dumbwaiter, throwing away any cartons, and loading the dishwasher. That was much less fun, but I did it.

The cafeteria job turned out to be a real advantage, though, because, before or after the rush, there was time when I could actually sit down in the cafeteria and eat. My breakfast, lunch, and dinner were all free. So not only did I get a little money, but my meals were taken care of. There were always a few people around, and they would often ask me to join them and talk about myself. They were very curious. I got to know some really nice people that way.

I remember the first time I asked for tea. The hot water came with a tea bag; I had never seen a tea bag—we had only had loose tea that we kept in a tin. So I looked at the teabag and just flicked open the bag, and the leaves floated around in the water. I thought, "Well, it's America. It's a curious way to drink tea, but . . . ." And then somebody said, "No, all you do is put the whole bag in the hot water."

That was just one of the many little mistakes I made.

TWO

CLIMATE CHANGE

I had just begun the academic year, and already felt completely stressed out, juggling the demands of the various courses and the requirement of maintaining a "B" average in order to keep my scholarship. It didn't help that I tried to take economics classes, as well as one called "The American System of Government," in which the first assignment was to read *The Federalist Papers*. The professor gave us one week, even though the book was around two hundred pages long. I was up every single night, surrounded by dictionaries, just trying to figure out the words. Plus, I had those part-time jobs.

I found myself having trouble with the language and following all of my lectures. Then there were the weekly quizzes. And, as if that weren't enough, I was informed that I also had to take a foreign language. That's when I went to the dean. "I am struggling with English," I told him. "English *is* my foreign language."

"No, no, that doesn't qualify," he said.

"How about German?"

"No, that's your native language."

"So, how about Latin or Greek?"

They looked at my transcript and said, "No, you've already advanced beyond what we teach in those two languages here at Duke."

I finally took French, which I had never studied before. This meant that I needed to translate the French through my German into English. I later learned that the initial purpose of teaching foreign languages at American universities was for students to be able to read the research in their fields in the original language, since a lot of it—medical books for example—weren't translated. Foreign language training, consequently, was not geared toward speaking. This was very different from the European tradition. In Europe, with the various languages overlapping, it was much more important to be able to speak the language, which was the aim of it being taught and seemed much more sensible, because ultimately, if you can speak the language, you can read it.

Ironically, for me at least, all freshmen were required to take an English 1 course, but I didn't qualify. Instead I was assigned to something called "English L"—for learners. The class included a kid from Venezuela, two kids who had fled Hungary during the Revolution of 1956, me, and almost the entire Duke University freshman football team. They were all wonderful people—all white, because the school was segregated then.

Our English professor—well, you couldn't really call him a professor—our *teacher* was brilliant. He was very good at teaching grammar. With my nine years of Latin and seven years of Greek, one thing I had learned was grammar. I understood grammar. So I became a star pupil not because I was speaking good English, but because I grasped the grammatical points really fast.

The class wasn't all drudgery though. Mickey Kun, one of the Hungarians, and I became good friends. When the holidays came around, Mickey and I were two of the very few students still on campus. I told him that in my family we had a Christmas Eve tradition: we would walk down to the church, about a twenty-minute walk (we never went to church except on Christmas Eve), sometimes in the snow, to the early evening service, in which children would perform. The program was usually pretty short and harmless. I wondered if there was something like that in Durham. As it turned out, the Christmas Eve service was a tradition for Mickey as well. So we started calling churches. Finally, somebody said, "Yes, we have a service at eleven o'clock." And they gave us the address.

We didn't have cars, so we had to hitchhike. When a car stopped, we got in and said we wanted to go to such-and-such address.

The driver said, "You don't want to go there."

"Why not?"

"It's right in the black part of town."

I said, "Well, you know this church?"

"Yeah, I know that church."

"All we want is to go to the church."

He dropped us off at the church. We walked in to find there wasn't a single white person. We were pretty hesitant, but the minister saw us standing all the way in the back and motioned for us to come to the front to sit down in the first row. He came down from the pulpit and asked us where we were from. We told him that we were Duke students, and that Mickey was from Hungary and I was from Germany. He said, "Welcome to the House of the Lord."

He went back to the podium, and he introduced us to the whole congregation. There was applause. The black people were much more lively than any white congregation I had ever experienced. The singing was fantastic. We had an absolutely great time.

A couple of weeks later, I read in the local newspaper that a black person, a very modest, shy woman, had shown up in a white church—probably a Baptist church. The woman did not sit down but was standing behind the last row. When the minister saw her, he walked all the way down the aisle, and told her to leave, shutting the door behind her.

So that was the climate in those days. That was the South.

THREE

SEPARATE, NOT EQUAL

I had some knowledge of race relations in American history: the Civil War, Lincoln, slavery, and segregation. However, until I arrived in Durham I did not know that North Carolina was segregated, nor that Duke University itself was segregated. I eventually learned that that was the reason why Duke didn't have more foreign students: the State Department would not allow an official exchange program to be associated with a segregated university.

Coming from Nazi Germany and its ideology of racial purity, it was difficult for me to process this idea of American segregation and figure out what I should do about it. By the time I got to Duke in 1957, there were already protests—led by Duke students—in Durham against segregation in movie theaters, restaurants, etc., but I chose not to participate on the grounds that I was a foreigner and I felt it was a domestic issue. (I now feel that I took the coward's way out, and I regret it to this day.)

In spite of student efforts to end segregation, the Duke Board of Trustees was not persuaded; they were behind the times, timid, conservative, and reactionary. (I remembered that when, much later, I became a trustee myself. It is the role of trustees to lead, not to follow.)

In the Durham movie theaters, blacks had to sit in the balcony, even while Duke students were demonstrating out in front. I found the fact that systematic discrimination against a particular group of citizens could exist in America—a country we Germans viewed as enterprising and modern—incomprehensible. Over the next few years, so many experiences of what it meant to live in a segregated South cropped up that would constantly catch me by surprise.

While I was working for the hospital's Dietetics Department (another one of my part-time jobs), because of its basement location, I got to know a black guy who worked in the boiler room. At first, we had great communication problems: my English was poor and his English—very Southern with an African-American lilt—was practically impenetrable to me. So we sat and smiled a lot. But eventually we got to know each other quite well. I don't remember his name, but I remember what he told me about his life. He had been in World War II as a soldier in the Pacific Theater. He told me that his son had become a professional baseball player—I believe it was with the Cincinnati Reds—and was a pretty accomplished person. I foolishly said, "Oh, did he go to Duke?" And then I realized immediately that he couldn't have attended the university because of its segregation policy. I apologized. He told me that he was fine with it.

That conversation made a big impression on me, because here was the son of an American soldier of World War II, who couldn't go to a university like Duke. And here was I, a German from recently defeated Nazi Germany, who could. The injustice of it was obvious and blatant. We never spoke about it and he was too polite to ever ask me anything about what had happened in Germany under the Nazis.

During my freshman year, Louis Armstrong and his band came to Duke to perform at the indoor stadium, Cameron, where they still play basketball. I was somewhat of a jazz fan and couldn't wait for the concert. In the stands above me I saw the segregated section where the black people—townspeople and university workers—were made to sit. They were allowed in, but they weren't allowed to mix or to reserve a better seat: separate but not equal. Nevertheless, Louis Armstrong had agreed to those circumstances. So I could see that even the black entertainers accommodated themselves to the South.

The concert was really fantastic, and afterward, I made my way to his dressing room. It was astonishing to me that there was so little interest among the students to meet him—after all he was a megastar of the era. I knocked on the door and walked in. And there was Satchmo Armstrong.

He asked, "How are you?"

I was star struck. I said my name. And I said, "I'm from Berlin, Germany, and I admire your work." Or something like that.

And he said, "Oh, Berlin! We were just in the Deutschlandhalle, you know, a few weeks ago."

He was a really cosmopolitan guy. We talked, and then he grabbed one of the big glossy programs that you could buy. He said to the band members who were with him in the dressing room, "Hey, listen, we have this kid here from Berlin! I want you all to sign your name under your picture!" He and Velma Middleton, the singer, signed their names as well. I still have the program. He wrote in big letters on the cover: "To my German Fans, Louis Armstrong." And below, in even bigger letters: "Satchmo."

Every once in a while, my roommate, Jim Whitlock, would take me home with him to Maxton, North Carolina. His hometown was one-third white, one-third black, and one-third Native American, and I saw how everything was segregated—three ways. The town had three separate benches, three separate drinking fountains, etc. Later, back at Duke, we heard that Maxton had hosted a Ku Klux Klan convention. It actually became a pretty famous incident because the Native Americans decided to have a little fun. They got dressed up in tribal costumes, got on their horses, and galloped into the barn where the Klan convention was being held. Whooping it up, they shot out the lights, shattering the light bulbs, and plunging the place into total darkness, confusion, and chaos. And then they left.

The Ambassador of JAZZ

Louis Armstrong
AND HIS CONCERT GROUP

My program autographed by Louis Armstrong, after his concert at segregated Duke University, 1958.

I personally witnessed other examples of racism. Once, a classmate invited me to his home. His family was very warm and friendly. They said, in essence, "Welcome! We want you to know that no Yankee has ever set foot in this house. And no Yankee ever will. But you are an honored foreigner—and by the way, that Hitler, he had sort of the right idea." I spoke up right away and told them I completely disagreed about Hitler. They dropped the subject. But that discussion confounded me—not only did they hate Yankees, but they were also total bigots.

At Duke's medical center, I met a professor of biochemistry, Professor Beard, who was like a god there because he had more research grants than anybody else. He asked me if I could teach him German. I said, "sure"—since he was paying well. So, on Sunday mornings I went to his farm outside of town. We would sit on the porch while I tried to teach him some German. He and his wife—who also worked at the medical center—had no children. I think the guy was basically pretty lonely and just wanted somebody to talk to. He never learned much German; we just talked. He was highly educated and talented at getting big grants, yet he had few social contacts. He had black maids and servants whom he treated with total condenscension—of course that was prevalent in the South; but he was a profound racist. He was absolutely convinced that the blacks were an inferior race.

It was confusing to me that American blacks, like my friend in the boiler room, had participated in the war effort that had defeated Nazi Germany, yet they were treated so shabbily at home. In spite of the African-American label, they were Americans first. It wasn't until I discovered old issues of a German newspaper that had been published during Hitler's time that I began to form an understanding about this "parallel injustice" between the experiences of the blacks and the German Jews.

FOUR

DISPATCHES FROM THE HITLER YEARS

The library at Duke was more conducive to studying than my room—of course, in those days, studying involved books instead of the Internet. So I spent a lot of time "in the stacks." Whenever I took a break, there were two things that particularly fascinated me. One was the periodical reading room. They had a whole room dedicated to newspapers from all over the world, as well as periodicals; they carried one or two German daily papers that showed up four weeks late. Every day, I would go to the reading room to see if I could get the soccer scores, albeit late. I would also read *The New York Times*. The second thing I did was check out the new books that came in each day. There was a hallway with a long shelf where all the new books were displayed. They were almost all hardcover, and I was fascinated to see the breadth of what they had in their collection.

At that time, the library had open stacks. You could wander through the stacks for hours. They were organized by subject matter, and one day I found some old German newspapers. The papers were not on microfilm; they were in the original. They were also not in boxes; they were attached to some kind of wooden spine. I discovered that these German newspapers were from the time of the Nazis—they were issues of the Nazi paper, *Völkischer Beobachter* (*The People's Observer*), dated from 1932 to the end of the war.

I was astonished to see them in the library's collection. (I learned later that someone had donated the newspapers to Duke.) The only disappointment for me was that they were the Munich editions, and so the local coverage wasn't about Berlin, which would have been more interesting to me.

At random, I started opening these papers, which covered the entire twelve-year Nazi era. Without fail, each paper had a screaming headline in big black letters, beneath which was a red bar. The headlines were almost always political, having to do with the latest accomplishments of the Nazi Party, or about speeches by Hitler and various successes achieved by Germany. These main headlines were never, to my recollection, necessarily racist. But the racism was there if you looked—maybe not on page one, but on pages two or three.

Since the Nazi Party published the paper, it was particularly vicious. Almost every day there were declarations of the latest restrictions on the Jews. For example, they had printed the announcement from the Minister of the Interior that "starting on such-and-such day, Jews would no longer be allowed to teach at universities" or ". . . no longer be allowed to work in their professions, in music"—all of that. The pieces were written pretty matter-of-factly. But the paper also published editorials that explained why the restrictions were necessary—and that's where the anti-Semitism was really blatant. On a regular basis, there were also all kinds of stories/articles about Jewish bankers and various crimes supposedly committed by Jews against humanity, and so on and so forth.

I continued to pull out copies of that paper whenever I had some time and ended up spending dozens of hours poring over the pages. I never read the issues in any really organized way; I kind of read them as I came across things. I was really curious. I wanted to find out how it had all happened. The issues covered the periods when Hitler came to power, when he was running the country, and when he committed all these crimes that supposedly nobody in Germany knew about. Was that really true? I guess I was also looking to better understand what my parents knew, what they should have known, or could have known. Here it all was, in black and white.

Even before discovering these papers, I knew that my father must have been aware of what Hitler was doing to the Jews. He clearly must have known that Hitler blamed them, especially the Russian Jewry, for a lot of things. I had to assume that if my father hadn't had some sympathy for the Nazis' prejudices, anti-Semitism, and nationalistic tendencies, he would not have joined the Nazi Party. And I knew that the material about the Nazis that was available at the time was pretty bad. After all, there was a blueprint of the whole thing in Hitler's *Mein Kampf.*

Hitler had written *Mein Kampf* in 1924, when he was a prisoner at the Landsberg Prison in Bavaria, and it was published in 1925. It was a bestseller in Germany, and, if you can imagine, once Hitler took power, his book was given as a gift to every couple when they got married. In *Mein Kampf* he made a lot of the fact that the Bolshevik Revolution was heavily Jewish; he always ranted and raved against the Bolsheviks.

When Hitler talked about the German Jews, it was in the sense that the Jewish bankers had caused Germany to lose World War I. Most Germans seemed to agree with that. There was a general sentiment among the German population—the non-Jewish German population—that Jews had a disproportionate influence over the banks and the media. After World War I, rumors spread that the Jewish banking monopoly had financed the Allies. (Even though, during World War I, there was really no particular reason why they would finance only the Allies.) There was no more obvious anti-Semitism in World War I on the German side than there was on the Allied side, and many German Jews fought very well in World War I—they were very patriotic, especially the secular Jews.

But that did not matter. Hitler basically said that the international Jewry—the banking monopoly—was squeezing Germany and taking every drop of blood out of the German economy. His use of the word "international" loomed very large. "International" in this context implied that the German Jews were against the German nationalists and that the Jews had no real home. As Hitler told it, their home was the world of money. And they couldn't care less whom they damaged, as long as they profited. (The Nazi propaganda machine said that it all had to do with money, and sucking the life out of ordinary people.)

In fact, for hundreds of years Jews were not allowed to enter professions other than money lending and a few other activities. They weren't allowed in government in Germany until the late nineteenth century. Even in Britain, there were prejudices. And they really had no choice but to get into these other professions; they became bankers. They had to work in an environment of discrimination, and still had to make money, which they managed to do quite well. Once they made the money, there was the feeling among the public that the Jews flaunted their wealth—such as buying big houses and fancy horses—and rubbed it in people's faces. That caused envy and resentment.

The non-Jewish people said, "okay, the Jews may have money, but they're socially not acceptable." It was very difficult for Jews to break into the "Old World" aristocratic society. That continued into the twentieth century, and it was one of the reasons why some Jews changed their names. Some even became Christians to gain a kind of social acceptance because money alone was not adequate.

The non-Jews, basically, were willing to do business with the Jews, but they did not want them in their homes. That attitude was considered "normal" anti-Semitism and was prevalent not only in Germany but also elsewhere. (France, for example, was always considered somewhat anti-Semitic—which came to light during the Dreyfus Affair of the late nineteenth century.)

I just didn't know how much of Germany's racist history my father knew at the time. He was a member of the Nazi Party—and that makes him a Nazi. To be called a Nazi, though, conjures up images of hatred and evil acts—and that wasn't my father. Yet, I couldn't fathom what went on in his mind. I remember hearing him say that, when he was in Vienna—and farther east—before the war, he had seen, for the first time, Orthodox Jews with their hats, beards, and *payos* (sidelocks). He said that he had laughed at how funny they looked, running around in their ancient black coats, and so out of touch. They were much more prevalent in Vienna than in Berlin. (I am not sure they even existed in Berlin at the time.) That may have been the genesis of his anti-Semitism: the Orthodox

Jews' "strangeness," and their inability to compromise with the rest of society—their exclusiveness. They were the ones who were caricatured by the Nazis, whose faces stood for the typical Jew. The Orthodox Jews were easier to vilify than others. There was always a certain feeling—probably part of the propaganda—that if they were in charge they would sure as hell discriminate against us; they would probably force their ways on us. It was a feeling that the Jews didn't belong to a modern European society. I think that was part of it.

As for my mother, I believe that she knew nothing about what was happening to the Jews, but she obviously condoned the anti-Semitism—again the long-standing "normal" anti-Semitism—which Hitler tapped into. She was also anti-Catholic. In almost equal degrees. She had very strong opinions. She would say, "The Catholics are all *falsch* (false), they are not straightforward." I believe that she ranted more against the Catholics simply because there were more Catholics than Jews; she didn't like the Vatican or the Pope. To her they were "foreign." And I think she also viewed the Jews as somewhat foreign. She was a woman of her times. But she never joined the Nazi Party; she was pretty much apolitical.

On the other hand, Uncle Hugo was vehemently opposed to Hitler and his ideals. I doubt that he hung the mandatory Nazi flag, and if the Nazis came to visit him to reprimand him I'm sure he said, "Look, I am a World War I veteran, don't bother me." The Nazis respected those who had served in World War I—up to a point. If you were—like Uncle Hugo—a non-Jewish veteran, particularly one with both legs shot off, amputated just below the knees, you were pretty much immune to harassment. Much later, Uncle Hugo told me that in the '30s he had some lively discussions with my father and another friend, Eberhard Kranz. Uncle Hugo would tell them, "This guy Hitler is a fraud. It's terrible what he is doing to Germany." And my father would say, "How can you say this? He is the savior of Germany." But later, they would toast each other with a glass of wine. Of course, Uncle Hugo wouldn't have been quite as open with my father if he hadn't completely trusted him—that sort of trust in those days was very, very rare.

During the war, I don't ever remember the subject of Jews coming up, but I was only three to nine years old at the time. Before the war, Berlin actually had an active Jewish community, the largest Jewish population of all the German cities. Even so, I didn't know that there were Jews living near us; I never considered who was Jewish or who was not Jewish. And it was never pointed out. After the war, my mother told me that the Linke family, who lived next door to us in Spandau, were Jewish—one quarter Jewish. Everybody had to submit evidence whether or not they were Aryan, but the Linkes somehow avoided this process. The family stayed throughout the war without any trouble. Nobody reported them.

When things were bad, you had to prove that your parents were not Jewish. I'm not sure how it was done. Your grandparents also couldn't be Jewish. And if somebody was a quarter Jewish, that was already too bad; they would be classified as Jewish. Any Jewish blood would get you on the list, which is why it was so rare for the Linkes to have no trouble. Aryan women married to Jewish men were a real problem for the regime.

There is an example of this from March of '43: When a group of Jewish husbands were arrested, their non-Jewish wives showed up in front of the prison that held them and demonstrated against the Nazis. They shouted, "We want our husbands back." This was in Berlin—and the Berlin population generally supported them, basically saying: "You know, this is ridiculous. They are married and they belong together." The party officials consented and they let the men go. The "Rosenstrasse protest" became one of the few cases of civil disobedience during the war.

There were hundreds of Jews who survived the war in Berlin. They were never deported because, like the Linkes, they weren't reported. They weren't necessarily in hiding. There were plenty of people—not only the Jews, but also those like my brother with the draft—who seemed to find ways to elude the system. Berlin, after all, was a Left-leaning city. (It still is.)

In the south of Germany you couldn't have gotten away with such a demonstration—or years of evading the authorities. Bavaria and Austria were the worst. Of course, they were also the places with the fewest Jews. In Berlin, people knew one another and there were many personal ties, friendships. I believe that's how so many survived, but I am not an expert on it.

Of course, the biggest question of all that kept gnawing at me as I read the newspapers is what the German people, my parents included, knew about the Holocaust. After the war, the subject was never brought up in school, as far as I can remember. Nobody talked about it. But I knew that there had been concentration camps, a Holocaust. That news had been published the second the war was over. The Allies made sure of that. One of their main objectives was to get out the truth.

Starting right after the liberation of the camps, the Allies ordered the German population who lived near the camps to visit them. The Germans— mostly women and children—were shown pictures and movies of the prisoners who had been killed. Yet some of those who had visited the camps still refused to believe that Germans had committed such atrocities. Because the Allied troops had herded them to the camps, they said that everything had been staged and that the troops themselves had probably done it. There were all kinds of conspiracy theories, even in the face of the facts.

Investigations by Germans into Germany's immediate past just didn't happen. There was no appetite for it. Many said, "Well, war is war." They said, "How many millions of civilians perished?" They said, "What happened to the Jews was just another really unfortunate part of this terrible war that we now want to forget about as quickly as possible." Everybody had been fighting for their own and their families' survival. Even for me, as a kid after the war, when I read in the papers about the camps, all those horrors blended together with all the other horrors of the war into one big horror. I looked at it in the same way that I looked at my city, which was completely bombed out.

As people coped with the after-war chaos, they hadn't yet grasped the whole significance of what had happened; the gravity and the politics of it didn't emerge until much later. It took twenty years, maybe, and the next generation—my generation—to reach adulthood for that to sink in. In the meantime, Germans began to distance themselves from the crimes. They saw that the biggest villain was Hitler—Hitler and his gang. People would say, "Hitler got us into this mess." Of course, the fact that they had voted for him didn't dawn on them. You have to recognize that almost everybody had been a sympathizer of the Nazis, whether they were members of the Nazi Party or not.

And then we heard, at the end of the war, that the Führer, while discharging his duties, had been killed; the reports implied that a bullet hit him or something and that Hitler had died a hero. But the Russians found his body, so I'm sure that the truth that he had committed suicide was published right away. However, by then, how Hitler died wasn't really important; he was dead.

My brother was very interested in what had happened during the war and dug around for the truth. He talked about all the ghastly things that the Hitler SS had perpetrated. In my brother's opinion, it was not a German problem so much as it was a problem of Hitler.

Jürgen, as I mentioned, was seven years older than I. When he was sent to the Hitler Youth camp outside of Berlin, a couple of the teachers strutted around in Nazi uniforms, and spouted propaganda. He was very upset about the fact that these same teachers were still allowed to teach after the war. After he was out of high school, he confronted them, since he was now beyond their reach. He laughed when he told me, "I finally told them off." And I said, "For heaven's sake, you can't do this; they are *my* teachers, too! I have to deal with them every day. Shut up, Jürgen!" I was still in school, and of course, the teachers knew that I probably knew. And so it was a dance, but the teachers never mentioned it.

In the late '40s and early '50s, while he was still in law school and living at home, Jürgen started assisting a German Jewish attorney—through an introduction from Uncle Hugo. The lawyer—his name was Eckstein—had immigrated to America. But after the war, he returned to Berlin and set up a very prosperous practice, working on gaining restitution for victims of the Nazi regime—the West German government was just beginning this process to compensate Jews and other victims. Most of the Jewish clients were those who had managed to leave the country, not Auschwitz survivors.

Jürgen wasn't the only one working at Eckstein's firm. There were other lawyers and paralegals. The work was lucrative for Jürgen and other lawyers there, because he got a cut of every settlement. They dealt with the German government, and all they had to do was get together documentation and present it in the right form. My brother became pretty wealthy in the process. So, in a way, it was a moneymaking operation, a fact about which Jürgen always felt some guilt. But I'm sure Eckstein saw that my brother was the kind of person whom he could trust with this work, and it was one of the reasons why he was sent to New York to get to know the clients better. Some of the issues, according to my brother, were very complex.[2]

Sitting in Duke's library, I was flooded with all these thoughts about that period, and my family's understanding of it. It opened my eyes to what had happened. It made me realize that my parents certainly had to know about the restrictions placed on the Jews, even if they didn't know the truth about the deportations to the camps. But they, like the majority of Germans, had tolerated them. It made me disgusted for being German. I immediately wanted to distance myself as much as possible from Germany. I told myself that Germany was the wrong country for me.

My feelings toward Germany changed dramatically, from the positive to the negative. I started looking at Germany from a more cynical perspective. I thought that Germans hadn't changed, that they couldn't be that different now. They had accepted all that happened—they may not have known the details about the concentration camps, but they had ardently followed the

---

[2]   When Jürgen was in New York, he worked for a different law firm, but I think it was an affiliate of Eckstein's firm.

Nazi Party. The Nazis won the election, the first election, fair and square. And although subsequent elections were a little bit manipulated—because the ballots had to be openly submitted—there was no question that the Nazis would have won anyway. The Nazis were enormously popular after Hitler came to power. It wasn't that they immediately realized he was a crook or some kind of a tyrant, or a dictator. On the contrary: the vast majority believed in him until the bitter end.

I saw the historical parallels that could be drawn between the two countries' experiences—especially the experiences of the American blacks and the German Jews—at least in theory. Blacks, of course, could still go to school under the "Separate But Equal" doctrine. If Hitler had treated the Jews as the Americans treated the blacks, things may not have been as bad. Don't get me wrong, I don't mean to say that I thought the situation of the blacks was an easy one. Lynchings were not unheard of during my time at Duke. A couple of them took place not far from Durham. The civil rights marches, and the famous lunch counter protests in Greensboro, NC, were yet to occur.

Anyway, I knew the Nazi disaster would be with Germans for generations. In hindsight, I felt—feel—ashamed. Who wouldn't, considering what Germany did? And it became evident to me that I should have been more curious. But my generation—the direct children of the generation responsible—was hesitant to ask questions, especially in light of the fact that our fathers had suffered serving during the war. It didn't seem fair for us to condemn them.

Before I left Germany, there was very little talk about guilt. The country was preoccupied building a democracy, which it had never experienced, except for the failed attempt between the two world wars. So, obviously, any Nazi party or any Nazi-like party was banned by the constitution. *Mein Kampf* was also banned in Germany until late 2015. The government was resolutely nervous about any comeback of fascism or Nazism. But, as I mentioned, they did not rigorously investigate the recent past.

In fact, it wasn't until fairly recently that it came out that the first West German chancellor, Konrad Adenauer, who by no means was a Nazi and was appointed Chancellor because he was *not* a Nazi, had many former prominent Nazis in his government—primarily because they had certain skills that he needed. So there was a tendency either to overlook certain crimes that had been committed by certain people—or to claim ignorance.

It took until the generation after mine for Germany to confront the guilt. The Germans have a word for it, which is *Vergangenheitsbewältigung*—one of those incredibly difficult German words. Literally translated, it means "mastering the past," or "getting a grip on the past." But that did not happen until after I had left Germany in 1957.

In the quiet of the library, I realized that I would have been happier if my father had never joined the Nazi Party. I had no doubt about it. I would be happier still if he had been active in the resistance. But then I probably would never have been born . . . so it's all sort of hypothetical.

FIVE

WHERE THE GIRLS ARE

By the time I had finished my first semester at Duke, I had more or less mastered English. The second semester turned out to be easier, but still pretty tough. And, when March of my freshman year rolled around, some friends invited me to go with them down to Florida, for what I had learned was the all-important "spring break."

The family of my friend John Pruner had a condo in Fort Lauderdale, a town where lots of college kids gathered for spring break each year. John and four other guys, including me, took turns driving John's convertible practically nonstop. We rode with the top down through South Carolina and Georgia, through fascinating little towns, and I began to love the music on the various radio stations we picked up. That was heaven!

When we got to Fort Lauderdale, the whole beach scene was fantastic. The main place to go was the famous Elbo Room, which always had a long line waiting to enter. It was basically just a shack on the beach with a bar. But it was a real bar that ran the entire length of the room. When you finally got to the front of the line and entered the Elbo Room, you ordered a drink or two as you were being pushed forward. When you got your drink, you would drink as much as you could, and by the time you were finished—after ten minutes or so—you would find yourself going out the other side. That was the place to go.

Spring break was an unbelievable experience. Nothing like it would ever have happened in Germany. And there were girls everywhere you looked!

I had my first kiss at the ripe ol' age of eleven, or maybe twelve. I know that it was after the war, in 1947, when I was taking violin lessons from a well-known female professional violinist; she had two daughters who were roughly my age, and from time to time her daughters and I would play chamber music together. I remember one night they came to our house for dinner, and afterward, because they did not live far away, I walked them back to their house. We were following a small path, and it was pitch black. All of a sudden, one of the girls kissed me on the mouth. My first kiss! But, to this day, I don't know which one it was. I was so dumfounded. You know, I really didn't even know what a kiss meant. But it got my juices flowing a little bit.

My social life with girls picked up when I was about fifteen years old and my parents sent me to dancing school. Initially, I was very reluctant. The dance teachers were the European champions in the Viennese waltz; this was not the minor league. We had to be well dressed. And it wasn't just that they taught us how to dance—in between dances, they taught us etiquette. For example, they explained what you do if you go into a theater and you have to pass other seated people before you get to your seat: you face them, and don't pass with your back to them. Dancing and manners were considered important to the educated upper class because there were a lot of social functions—formal dances—and you had to be able to do the different ballroom dances: waltz, tango, fox trot, rumba, and samba. Although at first I wasn't thrilled to have to attend, I enjoyed all this because there were some really, really sexy girls in dance class, and I had my eye on one of them. But, one day, my brother came to one of the dancing classes just to visit—he had taken lessons there a few years before me. He immediately started a conversation with the girl I was interested in, and she just adored him, because he was older, taller. I didn't stand a chance—she obviously didn't share my enthusiasm for our being together. Jürgen and I laughed about that later—the fact that we had similar tastes in girls.

My first and only serious girlfriend in Germany was Linde Unholtz. She was the daughter of the head of a hospital—the doctor who had administered my health exam for my visa to come to the States—and I think I must have met her at some sort of social event. By then, I was almost twenty years old. At about the same time that I learned that I was going to Duke, Linde learned that she had been accepted as a high school exchange student in Glenside, Pennsylvania, near Philadelphia—the same school that Sandy Calloway, the girl who had helped me with my college applications (and who, at fourteen years old, had piloted a plane solo across America), came from.

Dating in America was very different from anything I had experienced in Germany. In Berlin, you always went "Dutch." The boy never had to pay for the girl's expenses, or vice versa. And it wasn't up to the boy to ask the girl out. Often, I would get a call from a girl who'd say, "Hey, I've got an extra ticket for such-and-such theater performance. You want to go? Yes or no?" It was no big deal if you said no. Sometimes I would say, yes, and then she would say so-and-so was also coming along. It wasn't necessarily just her. It was all very ad hoc, which was actually very positive, I thought.

Instead, when I was at Duke, if I wanted to take someone out on a date, with hardly a penny in my pocket, I still had to pay for everything. To me, that was extremely old-fashioned. Also, the whole sexual thing seemed screwed up in America; America—when it was not on spring break—seemed like a very uptight society when it came to sexual mores.

To make things more complicated, Duke, in those years, had more boys than girls. Since dating was very important—Duke was always a bit of a social school—you sometimes had to seek out girls from other schools, like UNC or NC State, but then you were competing with their male students. Or you had to go to Meredith College, which was an all-girl Baptist college in Raleigh—but they weren't allowed to kiss, or even dance. So the competition was fierce to get a date. Guys would start calling weeks in advance. And, of course, considering the dating habits I was used to, I had no clue what was going on. Besides, I was too busy with my part-time jobs. But occasionally, someone would say, "You have to come to this party tomorrow. You have a date yet?"

I'd say, "No."

"Ah, you don't have a chance now," he'd say. "It's way too late."

However, I had gotten to know many of the student nurses at the hospital. Since they never knew their schedules, they could not commit to dates ahead of time, and on Friday nights some of the non-working nurses would often eat in the cafeteria. So I'd go to the cafeteria and say to one or another, "Would you like to go out tonight?" "Sure," she would often say. And I'd show up at the party, usually with a really attractive girl. The guys would ask, "Oh, where did you get her? You didn't have a date yesterday." And of course I knew enough to say, "I have my sources."

Pretty soon, they would come to me and say, "Can you get me a date?" I started asking other girls, and setting them up on blind dates. I became quite popular that way, and I was invited to live in the Theta Chi fraternity section of the campus—where my roommate Jim was already a member. Although I didn't join the fraternity, I got to participate in all their parties and social life. And it didn't take me long to become pretty comfortable with that life.

I realized just how much I was enjoying myself and wondered whether I should go back to Germany. In February—just before spring break—I went to the administration, and to my great surprise, they said, "You have a four-year scholarship." I wrote home and said that I really wanted to stay for another year and explained why. My parents were totally opposed to it. They felt that the American educational system was inferior and that I was just having fun, doing nothing serious. But I had never learned more in my life than in that year. In the end, I ignored their opposition because they didn't support me financially anyway.

The one thing I needed though was a summer job. I needed the money.

SIX

LIDO SHUFFLE

Wyman Yelton, a friend of mine at Duke, had worked at the Lido Beach Hotel on the south shore of Long Island, New York. He said that a lot of the kids at Duke would get jobs in local country clubs, watching the swimming pool, or something. But it didn't pay anything, so they lived at home. He pointed out that, since I couldn't live at home, I needed a real job. He told me that if I really wanted to make money, I had to go north. That's when he suggested the Lido. He also told me that it could be really tough to get a job because in '58 we were in a recession. But he said, "Go ahead and apply," and gave me the name of an employment agency in New York City.

I sent the agency their ten-dollar application fee, and shortly afterward they sent me confirmation that they had a position for me, so I felt pretty good about having a job lined up. They requested that I come to their offices in person as soon as school was out.

At the beginning of the summer I went up to Philadelphia and stayed with the Brecht family, who had hosted my German girlfriend Linde Unholtz during her high school exchange year. (Linde had already returned to Berlin.) I then took the Greyhound bus to New York. When I showed up at the employment agency and presented my piece of paper, they said, "We don't have anything."

I said, "You promised me a job."

"Yes, but there's a recession going on." It was all very hectic; they told me to sit down, and they would figure something out.

So I sat there. I sat there watching people coming and going, in and out; it was pretty interesting. The agency specialized in the hotel business, so there were chefs and line cooks; there were waiters; and there were all kinds of hotel personnel, all looking for a job in a hotel. I learned that the Lido Beach Hotel, during the off-season, maintained a staff that was all professional. But during the summer, the high season, they needed to hire a lot of people. The place was very exclusive and had a permanent golf club in addition to the main hotel for people who were mostly from New York City.

At lunchtime, I stepped out to get something to eat. That was difficult, because I had barely enough money for the bus fare back to Philadelphia. It was a very hot and humid day, so after I found something to eat I went back to sit in the office. By the end of the day, they repeated, "There's nothing today," and basically pushed me out the door. And that was it.

The next day, with my financial resources dwindling, I got on the bus again. The same thing happened. I showed my paper at the agency. They told me to sit down. So I sat down. I had nowhere else to go. After all, I was an unskilled student, looking for only temporary summer work.

At noon, I again went out. I had no money left for food, and I had no money left for the bus to go back to Philadelphia. I had maybe twenty cents in my pocket, which meant nothing in New York. I sat on a bench, in Central Park, and was feeling very depressed. I noticed that there was a group of people handing out pamphlets, advocating the Communist Party. I took a pamphlet and considered that capitalism was really unfair, and communism—where everybody is equal—may not be so bad. In that moment I felt that I was one of the oppressed. Of course, after my life in Berlin I knew better, but the feeling just came over me. It's the only time in my life that I even came close to considering communism as an option. I really felt sorry for myself.

Hungry and sweaty, I was annoyed with the whole situation and panicked about what I would do if I didn't get a job. I went back to the agency and sat until five o'clock when they said once more, "Nothing today." This time, however, I refused to leave. I said, "Look, I have no money left. I was promised a job. I sent in ten dollars. You've got to do something for me." I made a real nuisance of myself, causing a bit of commotion. I was told to go into somebody's office—maybe the manager's or the owner's. The man behind the desk said, "Sit down and tell me about yourself."

"I'm really desperate," I said.

He said, "You're from Germany, right?"

"Yeah."

"Where in Germany?"

"Berlin."

"Oh," he said. "I still have an aunt in Berlin." He explained that his aunt lived in Lichterfelde, a district of Berlin.

He was Jewish and very friendly, and he told me not to worry. He picked up the phone and called up the head waiter at the Lido's golf club. "Joe, I have this really clean-cut German kid here. He goes to Duke, and you gotta get him a job." They obviously knew each other well. He turned to me and said, "Go out to Long Beach, and look up Joe Alsop. He knows about you. And he'll take care of you."

Lido Beach Hotel, Long Beach, Long Island, NY.

Boy, was I relieved! I thanked him and then I stood there.

"Well, anything else I can do for you?"

"Yes, I don't have the train fare."

He reached into his pocket, and said, "No problem," and he gave me the fare for the train to Long Beach.

When I arrived, Joe Alsop (not the famous journalist from the mid-1900s, but another man with the same name) said, "I arranged for you to stay in the dorms, where all the help lives. You'll live there for the summer. Do you have any waiter skills or anything?"

When I told him that I had no such experience, he said I could be a busboy. "That is relatively simple. Just make sure people have ice water. And a lot of guests don't want butter, so don't give 'em butter if they don't want butter." (I found out later that that was a Jewish thing for those who were kosher. It was the very first time I heard about religion-based dietary restrictions.)

The golf club was a different work culture. The waiters were all men and they were professionals—as opposed to the wait staff in the big dining room of the main hotel, which was made up of female students. As for the guests, the first thing I noticed is that they all seemed to know one another. There was a lot of backslapping, and they were very loud.

Busing tables for a couple of hours a night was far from full-time employment. I needed more work. Alsop became my mentor. He asked me if I could swim. When I said, "Yes", he said, "Okay, you're a lifeguard. The beach lieutenant will show you what to do if something happens, and how to rescue people, and all that." The beach lieutenant cared only that I could swim. There was no further training. It was all pretty negligent. I still wanted more work. I asked around if there was anything else I could do. Somebody said, "You can shine golf shoes of the members." So my days and evenings were taken care of. Then there were the weekend nights.

The golf club had a terrace room, where there were weekend shows with major entertainers—big names, like Bob Hope. And so, on Friday and Saturday nights beginning at 11:00 p.m., I worked there, serving drinks and working a bit as a waiter since there wasn't much bussing to do at those shows. I worked until 2:00 a.m., after which I headed back to the dorm for just a couple of hours of sleep before my next job started at 6:00 a.m., or sometimes earlier.

My early morning job entailed my driving the hotel's VW bus, taking all the dirty linen to a professional laundry, picking up the clean laundry, and bringing it back. There were two of us doing this, and when we returned, we set the tables in the dining room for the coming night. By 8:00 a.m., I had to be on the beach.

I don't recall there being any shows on Sunday nights, and Mondays I had off—my only day off of the week.

Before I got to the Lido, it never occurred to me that all the guests would be Jewish. Germany had killed six million Jews, and I immediately thought of that when I went to the cabanas on the beach, and was surprised to see nothing but Jewish names on the nameplates: Schornstein, Schwartz, etc. I asked somebody, another non-Jewish employee, if everyone was Jewish. And he said, "Yeah, this is a completely Jewish hotel." I suddenly realized that that was why they used a Jewish-run employment agency. My co-worker added, "Not all of the lifeguards are Jewish, but all of the cabana boys are."

Being a cabana boy was the most lucrative job at the hotel—and one that was handed down from one family member to the next—because of the big tips they made bringing the patrons their newspapers and cigars. Cabana boys would sit down and socialize with the guests, which was out of the question for the rest of us. The cabanas had fancy furniture, and a couple of them actually had stock market ticker tapes running. It was pretty luxurious.

Lifeguarding at Lido Beach Hotel, 1958.

The Lido was considered the most elite Jewish resort in the New York area—more than any place in the Catskills. Many of the guests were lawyers or prosperous businessmen; they would commute from Manhattan, and some—at least the wives—would stay there all summer. All of them were successful enough to pay the resort's high rates, where the cheapest room in 1958 was fifty dollars a day (about $420 in present dollars).

Guests would inevitably ask me, "Hey, kid, what's your name?" And I would say, "Ingolf Mueller." And they would say, "What? Ing—, Ing—, what?" And, "Hey, can you spell that?" Then they would kind of look up and ask, "What are you? German?"

"Yes."

"Oh, okay."

That would be it. I could never tell whether their reaction was positive, negative, or indifferent. While several guests spoke with German accents—the German accent in itself was not a problem in that crowd; it was more a problem down South than in New York—I was still concerned because we worked for tips, and I was nervous that my background might affect my tip income. That was when I decided to call myself Karl. The name of my uncle and godfather was Karl-Heinz, and so I thought, okay, Karl's on my birth certificate somewhere along the line. And Karl was easier since it's not an unusual name in America. I also knew that Karl spelled with a "K" could be Scandinavian, or whatever. Ironically, Ingolf is not a German name. "Ing," which means young, and "olf," for wolf, actually is a Scandinavian name. I was named after a Norwegian pilot, a friend of my father who was killed flying into a church steeple, before I was born.

Once a week, the guests would hold a benefit—usually some kind of auction to raise money for a Jewish cause (either for Israel, or for a Jewish-American cause). The auction would take place right after the dinner. As a busboy I still had to be there, and stood against the wall and watched. One evening my eyes popped when I saw them raising $160,000 for some cause. $160,000 in a single night! That was unheard of. (That's like $1.3 million in today's money.) The whole thing was over in forty-five minutes. Thus, my first real exposure to Jews was not where they were the victims, but where they were the lords of the empire. That was probably a good thing for me, psychologically.

There wasn't supposed to be much contact between us lifeguards and the guests, but occasionally some of the younger guests would approach me on the beach to talk, because they were bored and they didn't have anything to do. I remember that first summer—I worked at the Lido the following summer as well—there was one particularly attractive girl, who said to me, "Oh, you're German. You can never be forgiven for what you did to the Jews. Never be forgiven."

I said, "You mean me personally, or Germany in general?"

"Germany in general, but also you personally because guilt like this carries forward through the generations. And you're just as guilty as the people who actually committed the crimes."

"Well, I don't accept that. That's like collective guilt, you know. And I had nothing to do with it, and Germany has changed."

"No, that's the way it is," she insisted.

After that exchange, she acted as if it had never happened. She was completely charming, and we talked about other things. It's not that she hated me and walked away, but she just wanted to let me know: "Boy, you are guilty. You know? Don't forget that."

I was taken aback because it was so out of the ordinary. Everyone was so polite. It was the only time that somebody pointed an accusatory finger at me—in fact, to this day—about Germany's role in the war.

At Duke University with leg cast from Lido Beach accident, 1958.

Among those American Jews, there were probably quite a few who came from Germany. As I learned later, the Jewish establishment in Berlin prior to the Nazis was not unlike the Jewish establishment in New York today. Jews were always more international, because they were bankers, mostly, as well as artists. So they were more cosmopolitan than the general public. They were at home in their respective cities; they were city people. Actually, other than the amount of wealth that was present at the Lido Beach Hotel, nothing really surprised me.

Overall, the summer went pretty well, except that, at the end of the season, I partially severed my Achilles tendon when I was caught by a wave as I was cutting lifelines anchored beneath the surf. I was taken to the doctor, and was in a cast for eight weeks.

Somebody advised me to sue the hotel for negligence, because we had been sent out into the surf with large kitchen knives instead of skin-diving knives. So I sued under the Workmen's Compensation Act.

A year later, a court on Long Island awarded me a nominal compensation amount. I took the money to the city and bought a copy of *The Complete Works of William Shakespeare*.

SEVEN

BACK AND FORTH

After the summer of my freshman year, I returned to Duke. Although it was too late to officially change the name Ingolf to Karl at registration, when I began working back in the hospital, I kept the name Karl, and became Karl Mueller. I felt acclimated to America, although, at Duke, being three years older than most of my fellow students and having a completely different background, made it sometimes difficult to fit in. And the school, in those days, made no effort to reach out to foreign students, perhaps because there were so few of us.

I started taking a couple of accounting and business courses with my eye toward getting an MBA. I had been interested in international business ever since the bank training program. Working in business was the family tradition, after all. My father had been an engineer and businessman, and, as I mentioned, my mother's relatives were all business owners—of smaller businesses of course. So a business career, I thought, would suit me just fine.

But I also continued to take other courses. College is not meant to make you a specialist. For somebody like me, it was very important to study political science and American government. I felt those were the things I would learn best in an American university. And I felt I could learn a lot about economics, since we had fabulous instruction. We had the first edition of a textbook by Paul Samuelson (the first American economist to be awarded the Nobel Prize), which I still have. I loved studying economics. Economics is not a science like mathematics or physics, but it pretends to be. It operates with a lot of mathematics, with a lot of hypotheses, assumptions, this and that. I especially found bringing several variables together into a model to be appealing.

My first economics professor was Juanita Kreps, who later became Secretary of Commerce under President Carter. She was a very good instructor. Even so, I'll never forget that during the class she would sometimes sit on the windowsill, showing off her beautiful legs. And she would turn to the class and say, "Whom do you like this weekend, Duke or UNC?" and then would continue to talk football for a while. That would have been inconceivable in a German academic environment, but it was so natural for her—a perfect way to open up to her students.

I loved how the American classroom was more personal, less rigid than I had expected. Sometimes a professor would invite us to his or her home. We'd sit around the fireplace and talk about the subject—or not. Later, when I went back to Germany and studied at the Free University, I sometimes attended classes in auditoriums with two thousand students, plus overflow rooms with screens set up, and loudspeakers. The professor would walk in like a god. He would stand at the lectern and read his paper, without ever raising his eyes. Everybody would take notes—and then he would disappear. Unlike studying at Duke, at the Free University you rarely had an opportunity to ask professors questions. They did not interact with the students, except in senior seminars in later semesters.

During the first two years I spent at Duke I never went home to visit; I couldn't afford it. My parents (mainly my mother) and I would exchange letters every couple of weeks. There was nothing wrong with my relationship with them, but I was grown up and Jürgen was back in Berlin. That was important to them—my brother was now the recipient of their attention.

The one person I did rely on for advice was Uncle Hugo. He not only steered me toward a business career, but was also supportive of my studying in America. And we often thought alike. He never had a son, so perhaps I was "the son he never had"—and in some ways he was the father I never had.

Once I started living in America, Uncle Hugo would write me regularly. He was one of the reasons why, later in life, I went back to Germany from time to time. Every now and then he would write, "It's been a long time. We have to have a thorough discussion about the economic situation in the world." When I would visit him, he would sit down at his desk in his home office, light a cigar, and we would share a bottle of Mosel wine or two. We would talk for hours. That never happened with my father, or mother. Uncle Hugo and I had these conversations until he died. He was a good listener, taking everything in. He gave good advice. When Mary Ellen—before we were married—lived in Berlin in 1961–62, and I was at Duke, I introduced her by mail to Uncle Hugo and his wife, Erika, who was a physician. He loved Mary Ellen and invited her to live with them for the year.

He knew he was responsible for me starting a business career, and he appreciated my later success more than my parents ever could. But he was no softie, either. He became quite wealthy during the re-building of Berlin, and he knew everybody. He was demanding, like most business people; yet he was proud of me. Whenever I advanced in business, somewhere in the back of my mind, I would say: "Uncle Hugo would approve of this."

The last time I saw him was in the hospital in Berlin in the 1970s; I had a general feeling that he wouldn't live until my next visit. I think he knew that, too. Yet we talked about business as if this was just one of many conversations to come. It clearly cheered him up. The visit was not emotional for him. It was very emotional for me, but I couldn't show it. When I left, it was casual, as in, "Well, I hope you get well soon—see you on my next visit."

There was to be no next visit.

When I told my parents I was staying for a second year at Duke, I hadn't wanted to upset them too much and said, "Okay, I'll come back after my sophomore year." But before returning to Germany, I worked for another summer at the Lido Beach Hotel—never mind that I was also suing them. I was made Beach Lieutenant, overseeing the other lifeguards. At the end of the summer, two friends and I began a tour of the entire continental US. One of the friends had graduated from Duke and was headed for graduate school at Stanford, so we took his car. After he dropped us off in San Francisco, the other two of us hitchhiked to Yellowstone National Park and then bought a really old car for $100 and drove it all the way back to the East Coast, without any insurance coverage.

From New York, I returned to Germany—as I had left—on an ocean liner. This time the American Friends Service Committee paid for my ticket, because I had gotten a job working as a chaperone for a group of ninety American and European high school exchange students that the organization was sponsoring.

Back in Berlin, at the age of twenty-three, I lived in the small house on my parents' property that had been converted from a storage shed. I studied at the Free University, where my brother had gone.

There were semester vacations—like three two-month periods a year—and during the first of those I was able to get a job at Coopers & Lybrand (now known as PriceWaterhouseCoopers, the international accounting firm). In Germany, the firm was known as Treuhandvereinigung AG. My bank training qualified me to help audit companies. They sent me to Frankfurt for two months, where I was on the team tasked to audit Hoechst, one of the three successor firms of IG Farben, the big chemical firm that the Allies broke up after the war. As a public company, Hoechst was required to have a certified public audit. My responsibility in Frankfurt was that of a junior auditor—as low a position as you can get. I primarily had to follow transactions, making sure they had been properly documented—that there were original vouchers and original invoices, and that everything was on the up-and-up.

The next semester break, I was in Hamburg, auditing a Dresdner Bank subsidiary called German South American Bank, for Dresdner's South American business. Hamburg is a big trading town, so while I was there,

I also worked on the audit of a large commercial shipbuilding company in Lübeck. And during my third two-month stint, I was in Berlin, where I was primarily involved with the audit of a brewery, Berliner Kindl.

I began thinking of studying for a year in France. I got on my Heinkel motor scooter and visited French universities, as well as universities in Lausanne and Geneva. In Grenoble, I visited my old friend Sandy Calloway, who was there at the time. In Paris, I looked up Nancy Voltz, whom I had met in Philadelphia; she was spending a postgraduate year at the Sorbonne, staying in the home of a countess near the Arc de Triomphe. Nancy was beautiful and vivacious, and I became smitten with her, which extended my time in Paris. In June of 1961, we took a five-day trip together. Driving her red Volvo, we traveled from Hamburg through northern Germany to Amsterdam, Egmond aan Zee, and Rotterdam—where she and her Volvo boarded the *Nieuw Amsterdam* for New York. Although I learned a lot during that time, nothing official came of my plans to study in France.

After two years, I said to my parents, "So now that I've studied here and I've studied over there, I really have an informed opinion, and I have to tell you that what I learned here was not as good as what I learned in the US. The universities over there are better, and I'm going back to finish school in the US." That was not at all easy for them to accept. I didn't mention to them that my recent friendship with Nancy had also played a role in that decision.

I was twenty-five years old, and after four years of university I had nothing to show for myself except a so-called *Vordiplom* (preliminary diploma) from the Free University. Duke had graciously agreed to give me credit for one of the two years studied in Berlin and to allow me to return for my senior year—with my scholarship intact.

I was once again on a US-bound ocean liner—and once again in charge of a bunch of high school exchange students, including a not-yet-famous Blythe Danner. It was August of 1961.

While we were on the high seas, we learned the momentous news that the East Germans had sealed off the border between East and West Berlin. We found out about it from the one-page news bulletin that was distributed on board daily.

I can't say I was surprised when I read the bulletin. Earlier that summer, one of the American high school exchange students and I had visited a camp in West Berlin for recent refugees from East Germany. It was overflowing. When we asked why there was such a sudden increased influx of refugees, they said: "Don't you know, they (the East German government) are going to close the border!"

I later learned more details: the GDR had blocked all movement between West Berlin and the rest of East Germany, initially with a barbed wire fence and then by constructing a wall that encircled West Berlin—a hundred and fifty kilometers (nearly a hundred miles) long. Next to the East German side of the wall there was a cleared strip of land that was studded with landmines, and on top of the wall there was piping and barbed wire. Every two hundred meters or so, there was a watchtower with armed guards. On the other side of the cleared strip there was more barbed wire.

When our ship—the *Berlin*—docked in New York a few days later, reporters and camera crews swarmed aboard, no doubt because of our ship's name, since the Berlin crisis was the number one news topic around the world. We learned from the reporters that Russian and American tanks were facing each other at the West-East Berlin border. It looked like World War III could break out any minute.

The ship's captain knew me because I was leading a large group, and he knew that I spoke decent English and had just come from Berlin. So he sent the reporters my way. In the ship's lounge, I gave interviews as though I were a big shot. One interview aired on CBS Radio News while I was still on-board ship. I never heard it. But I do have clippings from various newspapers that published my interviews.

The whole thing seemed surreal, because I hadn't even stepped back on US soil yet. The other thing that complicated matters was my responsibility for the exchange students. They had to be organized to meet their transportation needs from New York Harbor to various places across the US. A young lady from the American Friends Service Committee came on board to help me. Her name was Mary Ellen Terrell, and we met for the first time amidst all the commotion. The date was August 17, 1961, and two years later—to the day—we were married.

Mary Ellen generously shared her own memories of our first encounters with Marc Rosenwasser.

I first heard of Ingolf through our shared Philadelphia connections from the American Friends Service Committee. When I arrived in Philadelphia to work for that Quaker organization, everyone was talking about "Ingolf," as if he were a treasured part of everybody's family. One day, a friend of mine received a letter from him, which said something like, "I have one big regret. When I was at Duke, I was working so hard, and studying so hard, and with all these night jobs, I didn't get a chance to read Shakespeare in the original, only in German. Now I want to read the tragedies in the original. But I need a guidebook." And so my friend said to me, "Mary Ellen, you were an English major, and your father was a Shakespeare professor, why don't you help us?"

I looked at my friend and said—I swear to you, it's true, "I will go out on my lunch hour and buy A. C. Bradley's Shakespearean Tragedy, *and I'm gonna marry this man."*

I had heard from everyone that Ingolf was a real survivor. I learned all about the things that he'd done at Duke, about how he got these great grades, that he was a problem solver, and that he was a very, very hands-on kind of guy. I thought, "My god, he's the perfect combination!" I mean, he sounded as though he possessed all the qualities that I grew up with and valued: a sensitivity to literature and ideas, and the toughness to thrive under difficult circumstances. I had only seen a picture of him—one single picture—but I could see from his appearance that he was a real mensch; *he wasn't a gnome. Of course my friends laughed. But they stopped laughing when I applied for a job in Berlin, thinking he would be there; I didn't know he was coming back to the States!*

My plan was to resign my job in Philadelphia, get a job in Berlin, and then learn German. I didn't tell my parents the full reason why I was going over; I told them I wanted to study abroad, which made sense. At that time—this was 1961—there were two places I thought must be really interesting: Beirut and Berlin. That was my feeling. Berliners spoke German, which was easier to learn than Arabic, and Berlin had Karl—or Ingolf as he was known then. Of course, he was completely unaware of my plans, or of me. He had yet to hear my name mentioned. I know it sounds impulsive, but I always looked at things from all sides. And I thought that even if I went to Germany and found out that Ingolf was a complete jerk, I'd be in Berlin—a very exciting place. (Just HOW exciting I was yet to discover—after the wall went up!) So I applied for the Friends Service Committee program in Berlin, got the job, bought a "Beginning German" text, and was booked to sail in six months.

Perfect! Except for one hitch: Two weeks before I left, my friends got word that Ingolf had decided to come back to the States and take his senior year at Duke . . . . Well, I was packed, my bridges were burned, and I thought, "You win a few, you lose a few." I figured it was not meant to be. However, four days before I was to leave I did meet Ingolf when his ship came into New York—on August 17th, a few days after the wall went up.

He was chaperoning a group of returning American and new European high school exchange students to the US—our mutual friends from the American Friends Service Committee had arranged this for him in exchange for their paying his passage; they knew he would do a good job. And since I was also employed by the same organization, I had to meet the ship to assist the exchange students—that was my job.

So that was literally the first time I saw Ingolf. I went up to him and I said, "I'm Mary Ellen Terrell, and I'm with the AFSC, and I'm going to help you with the students." It was very businesslike. But . . . I really liked the way his mind worked from the very minute I met him. Ingolf now has no recollection of that first meeting, nor should he. We were both very busy and talked for maybe ten minutes to coordinate our separate strategies for getting our students introduced to their new host families in the area and to get others onto trains to the Midwest and planes to the West Coast. Afterwards, there were four more days that we spent outside of Philadelphia at Pendle Hill—a Quaker retreat—where the newly arrived European students who were staying in the area would meet with the American students who had just arrived back from abroad. It was a kind of orientation and de-orientation for the two groups.

There were sparks between Ingolf and me . . . despite everything . . . despite the fact that the timing was completely discouraging. We were going to be separated for a year. I think I kind of fell in love. And it turns out, he kind of did, too. I remember every single thing he said during those four days, and how he acted. I remember watching him discuss politics with a German student; and the way Ingolf talked and listened to the kid with such dignity and respect I thought was great . . . just subtle little things. And especially, I remember one evening at Pendle Hill; he and I and a friend were sitting around after dinner, and I was telling Ingolf about my plans to go to Berlin.

He said, "Well, how old are you?"

"I'm 23."

"So you're going to go to Berlin for a year. My experience from the girls at Duke is that they all are just frantic to get married; that's all they have on their minds." And then he said, "Aren't you afraid that you'll be on the shelf?" (At the time, this expression referred to women who were out of the main stream of being available to wife-seeking men.)

I'll never forget that—such a direct question. I thought, "Here is somebody who's a real person, who doesn't have a 'line,' who talks to you without all this game-playing, this girl-boy, man-woman game playing" (which was very common in the '50s and '60s.)

In those four days we got acquainted, but outwardly it was strictly business. However, he did offer to take me to my ship in New York. My parents had come from Oregon, and my sister was there, and everybody came to see me off—probably wondering why I had chosen to spend so much of my time with this total stranger instead of them. Later, I wrote Ingolf a letter from the ship, and he answered immediately. We kept writing each other; the letters flew back and forth for ten months. And by mail, we truly fell in love.

I finally found myself on firm ground in New York after that hectic day in August of 1961, when I had given all those "expert" interviews on board the ship with my exchange students. Life continued at a fast pace. I reconnected with Nancy Voltz, who now lived in New York and worked for Chase Manhattan Bank. (I wouldn't see Mary Ellen again for another two days, and only then did sparks begin to fly.) Also my Duke roommate, Jim Whitlock, showed up in New York. He had graduated and had decided to spend a postgraduate year in Berlin. I put him on the same *Berlin* that I had arrived on, and he sailed on August 19, 1961. Jim had already spent his junior year in Munich, and his German was excellent. He also knew Spanish well. (Later, he added Danish—because of a Danish girlfriend—French, Swahili, and probably other languages to his repertoire. He entered the Foreign Service and served with distinction for many years. He and his wife Carol are still among my best friends.)

Then it was off to the Quaker retreat at Pendle Hill, outside Philadelphia, for an orientation session for the European-bound high school exchange students. In that idyllic place I got to know Mary Ellen better, and an attraction unlike any other I had ever experienced began to develop. But there was no time, not even two days, before she was to go to New York—and then Germany. I decided to go on the students' bus with her to New York. We visited Greenwich Village and the Statue of Liberty. There was a farewell party for passengers, friends, and family on board the *Bremen*—and then she was gone.

I didn't know what to make of it. My rational side told me that I wouldn't see her again for perhaps two years and nothing could possibly come of it; my emotions told me otherwise. But, for the time being, there was nothing I could do but complete my senior year at Duke.

As I started my senior year, I stayed in the Bell Building, which was part of the medical center. My job there was to be the night watchman, which included inspecting various rooms, checking on medical devices that ran during the night, and keeping an eye on the animals used for medical research. Seeing those animals was often heartbreaking, because some of them were almost in mid-surgery, often with insufficient pain medicine. At the same time, I also did statistical correlation analysis on chicken experiments, though I don't remember the purpose of it.

I was the only one living in the Bell Building. My room was a converted lab, and mail was delivered into a rack that was visible through the frosted glass separating my room from the hallway. If a letter came from Mary Ellen, I could identify it through the glass by its distinctive airmail border, and even though I would try to sleep in because I had been up all night, the sight of those airmail envelopes made me jump out of bed, get dressed (the hallway outside was busy with lab technicians), and grab the letter. Thus, I fell in love with Mary Ellen— by mail. It was quite remarkable, and I couldn't explain it to myself: pretty soon a letter from Mary Ellen meant more to me than the physical presence of Nancy, who was still my "official" girlfriend and who, when possible, came to Duke—and whom I visited in Philadelphia for Thanksgiving and Christmas of 1961. Nancy's parents had even visited Nancy and me earlier in the year in Germany—and Nancy herself—made some unmistakable noises at Christmas about us getting engaged, which caused me to panic. After that, I allowed the relationship to cool off and die, as I focused on my airmail deliveries.

Mary Ellen: *I arrived in Bremerhaven where the ship came in. When I looked around, I saw familiar newsreel-like street scenes—all those streetcar lines—and all I could think of were the pictures, the black-and-whites, of Jewish children being rounded up for deportation and murder. At that time I found Germany really scary; it was only sixteen years after the war.*

I grew up as a child seeing those images, and I still can't envision them today without a very negative feeling about that part of Germany. I knew that there were many, many sides to the German character, and that, of course, you can't just judge everybody by the horrible thing that happened. But . . .

After I reached the Goethe Institute in Rothenburg [in southern Germany], where I was first to take an intensive language course for two months, I wrote to Ingolf. I told him that because of the history, there were things about Germany that frightened me. That when I talked to people, even really nice people in the street or the family whom I lived with, I was always kind of listening for anything that might betray their prejudices.

He wrote this wonderful letter back, in which he explained that he felt exactly the same way! He said that he was horrified by the Holocaust and by Nazism—and everything that that meant; and horrified that such evil had been perpetrated on innocent people. He wrote that he had come to the realization that he was born in the wrong country at the wrong time. [He explained that] if he could change his nationality he would—which later he did.

As I read his letter I thought about how good it was that he expressed himself in writing and basically put his guts down on paper. Somehow, I don't think if we had been sitting together on a sofa someplace, he would have opened up the way he did.

When it came to my family, Mary Ellen did her own bit of detective work while she was living in Berlin in 1960–61. Through long, separate conversations with my mother and brother, and even my father, Mary Ellen uncovered details about my family's perceptions of Hitler—which she shared with Mr. Rosenwasser.

While I was in Germany there were some things that I probably learned about Ingolf and his family that Ingolf himself didn't even know—at least in those days. I spent a lot of time with his family, having been introduced to them by mail from Ingolf.

Ingolf's mother, Erika, became my best friend. She was easy to get to know; she was always very open. When she talked about the war, she said that she was very naive about what was going on; she thought Hitler was fine. But when she saw Jews wearing armbands, she was shocked. I don't think she had any idea of what was happening to them. If she did, she never told me. She was out in suburbia and she had her kids, and spent her time worrying about taking care of the family. She told me that she didn't read the newspaper; she hadn't read, for instance, even that teachers were losing their jobs. I think she was just "Little Holly Housewife."

After Ingolf and I were married, and Ellen, our first child, was born, Erika came over to visit us in Philadelphia. One evening, after dinner, Ingolf confronted his mother about the war years, and about Nazism.

Ingolf said, "Well, didn't you know? Why didn't you know?"

"You know, we didn't, we didn't—," Erika said.

"Why didn't you educate yourself? Didn't you ask questions? Didn't you read papers? How could you not have known what was going on? When things were really happening, and you knew that this was a terrible time, why didn't you do something? How could you just go along with it?"

She said, "You know . . . survival. I wanted to keep you alive. What was I going to do?"

And Ingolf said, "Why didn't you leave the country, leave when you thought these things were going on, why didn't you get out?" Of course, I knew that Ingolf was well aware that it hadn't been that simple.

The whole scene was awful. I realized that that sort of conversation had never taken place before. I have no idea what provoked it then, but all this stuff sort of exploded. To this day, I feel guilty that I didn't step in and protect her from him. Erika was crying. But it somehow got resolved with hugs and apologies. And I don't think Ingolf ever, ever, ever really blamed her. I think he had a lot of pent-up emotions—and certainly those questions had been haunting him for a long time.

As for Jürgen, I could see that he felt so much guilt, just being a German. At fourteen years old, he read Mein Kampf; *he said that he confronted his parents about it [they had not read it], but they brushed it off as just rhetoric, not to be taken seriously. He was mature beyond his years.*

After the war ended, there was some program, an international program or something, where German youths could go to other countries to help the farmers in their fields—a sort of "paybacky" kind of psychological thing. So Jürgen went to Norway to work, but he had bad asthma and could hardly breathe; he was in bad physical shape. He completed the program though. That was before he received his law degree and started working on Jewish restitution cases.

He told me that he felt terribly guilty about making money by handling those cases. Of course he wasn't taking money from the clients. I think a lot of it came from the government, or whatever. But still, he said, just the whole thought of it was just like blood money, "dirty" money, somehow. On the other hand, he was doing really good things for all these people. But he always felt guilty about it.

Jürgen also talked about how difficult it was when his father returned from Russia. The father just assumed he was back in control; he was the patriarch and everybody would click their heels together. But Jürgen, Gisela, and Ingolf were no longer children; they weren't going to sit in the seats in the "kinder zone." So Jürgen said that he spent a lot of time trying really, really hard to communicate with his father—man-to-man, just the two of them. And Werner, their father, would not open up. He wouldn't talk about the war, the politics. Jürgen went further. He asked him questions like: "What did you think about Hitler? Did you know what was going on? What was your impression of what was going on? And couldn't you see? And how do you feel now, now that you know? And when did you know? At what point did you know what the Nazis were doing?" [Asking all]these questions—similar to the ones that Ingolf asked his mother years later—was like asking, "Where was your soul? Where is your soul now?" He verbally took his father by the collar, but could not get past step one—ever. Jürgen would say, "You've got to open up. Tell me anything; I don't care. But just talk to me." There was never any real communication.

It was very painful—not only for Jürgen but also for Werner. It wasn't in Werner's nature to be forthcoming, the way Jürgen's mother was. Werner was polite, and he had a nice (old) jolly sense of humor. He could have been just anybody at a cocktail party, making small talk. That was the way he was.

Mary Ellen gained what was perhaps the sharpest insight of anyone I knew into what was obviously my father's deeply held anti-Semitism.

Werner and I were sitting and talking a bit about our backgrounds. I told him about my time at Earlham College, and how naive I was, because I was from Oregon. When I went to Earlham, a Quaker college, originally, the school had something like a twenty percent Jewish enrollment. Many of the Jews came from New York and had gone to Quaker private schools before Earlham. And so the first guy I dated was Mike Wieder. We had a great friendship. At one point, I asked Mike whether he was a Quaker. And he looked at me and laughed, and he said, "Look at this face! You're asking me if I'm a Quaker?" And then I realized that, coming from McMinnville, I had probably never seen a Jew before. Anyway, I told Werner this.

He said—and I remember this well—he said, "You dated a Jew?"

"Oh yeah," I responded. "He was very good-looking, and really great." [I was probably baiting him a bit.]

And Werner said, "A Jew? They're ugly. They wear those weird hats and curls down their faces." And boy, that told me everything. He may have been outwardly polite, but he was a real anti-Semite. It disgusted me. It didn't come as a shock though because there were a lot of things about which he was just clueless. Yet it's one thing to be clueless, and another to be truly anti-Semitic.

Uncle Hugo, who was famously anti-Hitler from day one, told me that shortly after the war began he said to Werner, "Do you know what's happening to the Jews?" And Hugo described to him what he had seen. He had been on a train, which had passed close enough to one of the major concentration camps that he saw—I don't know whether he had binoculars or whether he could see it with the naked eye—the barbed wire fence and the prisoners, emaciated, standing behind it. "When these Jews are put on cars, this is where they're going." Apparently, Werner just brushed it off. "Oh no, you can't be right, that can't be right. That can't be happening. No." And he just wouldn't listen. Perhaps he didn't want to believe Hugo; or maybe he knew, and he didn't want to admit it. These are things we'll never know. The family always described Werner as being very naive. Just child-like naive, even though he was brilliant.

They said that Werner never talked about his POW experiences, but he did make one observation to me. He said that he was one of the oldest *prisoners—he was already in his forties when he went back into the war. He was housed with the other officers, most of whom were much younger than he. And the death rate was much higher among the younger ones than the older ones. His take on that was that he, Werner, and the other older prisoners had families who needed them, whom they desperately wanted to return to—a real-life incentive. His whole goal was to be able to live to get back home, to be the father, and to take his role, and to save his family. Many of the younger officers simply didn't have a place to go back to—or wives and children who needed them.*

For my generation, the generation who were children during the Nazi years, trying to understand what happened and why it happened—to our families, to the rest of the population, to the millions of victims of war and extermination—and to know that the German country was responsible, the country we were born in, whether we liked it or not, is a burden that will never be lifted. Every one of us lives with that guilt and shame, just like the Jewish girl at the Lido told me.

In the fall of 1961, Henry Kissinger spoke at Duke. I believe he still taught at Harvard at the time, but he was also an advisor to President Kennedy. He talked about Berlin and claimed that the US government had been absolutely unaware beforehand that the wall would go up.

After the lecture, there was a reception nearby. I told him that I had recently come from Berlin. I told him of my visit to the refugee camp, and that everybody had expected that the border would soon be closed. But he persisted that the US government had no advance knowledge, which led me to believe that either US intelligence was completely incompetent or that he did not speak the truth. I now believe that it was the latter—politicians have a complicated relationship with the truth. Or he wasn't close enough to the government at that time and didn't really know what was going on, but wouldn't admit it.

With Henry Kissinger at Duke University, 1961.

And at a board meeting of the American Academy in Berlin in New York, 2008.

I connected with Henry Kissinger again much later, when we both served on the board of the American Academy in Berlin and later became co-chairmen. I found him privately to be a very engaging individual, with a great mind and a self-deprecating sense of humor.

During my senior year at Duke, a professor said, "You should go to graduate school, get an MBA. We can get you a full scholarship at the University of Chicago." At the time, the University of Chicago had given Duke carte blanche for their professors to pick one student who they thought was qualified for a scholarship. It was very enticing. The University of Chicago had the legendary "free-market" economist Milton Friedman—it was a highly quantitative program, studying econometrics and the like. Chicago was academically very rigorous; it also had a reputation of training future academics, however, which was not my cup of tea.

Then Harvard offered me a full scholarship as well. They had one called the "Burlington Knitting Mills" scholarship, which was designated for one student from North Carolina (I was, by then, considered a North Carolinian) graduating at a North Carolina university.

I went to Harvard and talked to them. Of course, that was very interesting. Harvard even then was considered to have probably the best business school in the country. They said, "Look, there is a gentleman's agreement included in this scholarship that, after you get your MBA, you will return to North Carolina. If you don't do it, nothing will happen, but we ought to tell you that that's what Burlington Industries desires. They want you to do something good for North Carolina, because that's where they are based." So I took that into consideration.

In the meantime, somehow, Wharton, the University of Pennsylvania's business school, found out about all this, and they approached me and said, "We would like you to fly up to Philadelphia." They also offered me a scholarship, to their program, which was heavily geared towards finance. It was also one of the best business schools in the country, but I was even more intrigued because Mary Ellen would soon be coming back to Philadelphia. That factor clinched the deal with Wharton.

Duke's graduation took place on June 4, 1962. Weeks—maybe months—earlier, I had written both my parents about it; I told them that college graduation was a big deal in the States. I knew they didn't have a lot of money, but I hoped that they would come. They never wrote back. They just weren't interested. I think they still were of the opinion that I was doing something in America that they didn't really approve of—and they didn't understand why I wasn't studying in Germany. So when graduation came, it just came and went.

I was hurt a little bit by their dismissal. I couldn't help it, because everybody else's parents had come—their relatives and everyone else. I had nobody. Fortunately, I had some good friends, who invited me to their dinners and the other activities associated with the graduation.

In the end, I realized it was probably for the best that my parents didn't attend. Because of their limited English, the visit would have been a challenge for them—as well as for me—and there would have been too many things that would have needed explaining.

EIGHT

THE SUMMER OF '62

Once I had graduated from Duke and had the summer open, I decided to contact Coopers & Lybrand, the second-largest accounting firm in the country, at their Philadelphia office. I let them know I had worked for their German division. They hired me for that summer between college and graduate school, and not only did they hire me for the summer, but they hired me as if they expected me to stay. They put me in a very intense four-week training program at Drew University in New Jersey, which was set up to prepare trainees to go out to their clients and do auditing work.

By autumn I was ready to start the MBA program at Wharton. But, in the interim, something exciting was going to happen that I had looked forward to all summer: I was going to go back to Berlin—and return to Philadelphia with Mary Ellen in late August. She had decided to return to the States.

In July, Mary Ellen's sister Nancy, who lived with her husband in Philadelphia, and I went apartment hunting, to find an apartment for Mary Ellen. I knew that I would stay at Wharton's MBA House on Chestnut Street, and I wanted her nearby. Nancy came along because nobody would have accepted me—a German graduate student—renting an apartment for a single girl who was still in Europe. Mary Ellen's budget was sixty dollars per month—a tough proposition even in those days—but after two days we found a studio apartment a few blocks away from where I would be living.

On August 19 and 20, I went back to the Quaker retreat in Pendle Hill for another orientation session. I had once again managed a free passage by chaperoning exchange students. This time, we sailed to Europe on the *Bremen*. On the 29th, in Berlin, I saw Mary Ellen for the first time in more than a year. It was a bit awkward. We had barely known each other in person, but our letter-writing romance had advanced so far that now the reality had to catch up with it.

Mary Ellen was still staying with Uncle Hugo and Erika (his wife), while I stayed at my parents' house—which meant that the two of us were seldom alone. And, of course, she was still working, having become actively involved in risky cross-border humanitarian smuggling operations since her arrival in Berlin.

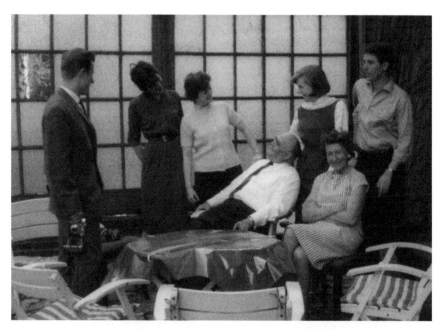

Uncle Hugo and his wife, Erika, seated, and Mary Ellen, standing, center.

In Mary Ellen's own words:

After two months of language training in Rothenburg, I arrived in Berlin in October of 1961, and I was immediately approached by several people who had spotted me at a student meeting that I attended in order to meet people. They said they wanted to use my passport to get someone out of the East. They said, "We know a girl who looks enough like you to get her out on your passport; just lend it to us."

The wall had just gone up, and almost everyone was doing something to try to ease the situation. I didn't give my passport up. I found out from the American Consulate that if someone got caught with my passport, I [would be] deported. Yet, I became involved in helping out in other ways.

I started going back and forth between West and East Berlin—as an American; it was relatively easy to get through the checkpoints—mostly taking messages to people. Even family members who lived only two blocks away from one another were now divided by the wall and had an impossibly hard time communicating. For example, in order to telephone from East Berlin to West Berlin, the call had to go through Frankfurt, and then it had to come back. And every conversation was listened in on and monitored. It was very difficult.

So, in the West, people were working hard to get family members, or lovers, or friends out of the East, and they would send people like me across with messages to specific people.

At the time, we "border crossers" had a student friend named Joel Baumann, who was from Israel but whose whole family, in Berlin, had been killed during the Holocaust. He had a lot of rage in him. He had returned to Berlin as a student, and he proved to be a great help to people like me. Every morning he went through one of the checkpoints and would be so confrontational that the East German border police would always choose him for whatever kind of search they were doing that day—the search would vary from day to day; each morning, a message would go out to all border guards, saying, for example, "Today is a handbag [or clothing, or body] search. Joel would come right back to the West and begin a chain of phone calls telling everyone what the search for the day was. So if it were a handbag search I would quickly sew such things as cigarettes and coffee—things that were used as currency—into the thick lining of a big coat I wore. I also took heart medicine to a woman who could not get it in the East. . . . The guards never varied from their orders. The messages from West Berlin family and friends, however, would always be delivered verbally.

I took these risks because my heart was breaking for the people who were separated, and whose lives promised to be so awful. I really wanted to help them get out. I had grown up in a Quaker family, so we were constantly thinking about global events and the plight of peoples around the world, although, until Berlin, I had never been physically involved in any sort of political action, no street marches—only a lot of behind-the-scenes stuff. In the summer of '58—that was prior to the creation of the Peace Corps—I did a summer "work camp" in a small village in Mexico with the American Friends Service Committee, helping to vaccinate people, to create a library, and, in my case, to set up a program for first-aid education for all of the villagers, young and old. But that wasn't really political.

Mary Ellen, smuggler between East and West, 1961–1962.

Now, in Berlin, I had done my homework, and I knew that, as an American, if I were caught, I wouldn't have received more than a two-year prison sentence. According to ex-offenders, the prisons in East Germany were "okay."

Actually, there was a fair number of Americans who were arrested. It wasn't publicized because neither the American nor West German government wanted any big blowups over something like that. I knew of somebody who got an eight-year sentence for something more serious than delivering messages. Whether he served the full sentence I'll never know.

I went back and forth probably three times a week over the course of the year—something like 150 times. I wasn't as afraid of getting caught with something on me as I was of getting shot. There were these border guards, these scared kids with pimply faces and huge dogs and machine guns at the one S-Bahn stop in East Berlin where only passengers from the West could get off and on the train, because East Berliners were barred from the area. In that underground station, the beams and support columns were all made of what looked like steel. I thought, "If one of these kids with his machine gun gets scared and starts firing, the bullets will ricochet off all that metal and it will be like being caught in a blender."

At the end of my year in Germany, Ingolf came to Berlin; he was chaperoning the 1962 batch of new and returning AFSC exchange students. We had not seen each other in a year, after having been together just four days. Ingolf arrived in Berlin in early evening and, perhaps before even going home to see his parents, came bounding up my front steps with a huge smile and a single rose that he had just swiped from the neighbor's garden.

Needless to say, we were both very exited and delighted to see each other again, laughing and talking non-stop. The next day, I was invited to his family home for lunch, where we all, of course, spoke German together. This was a first! Ingolf and I looked at each other—astonished—and laughed, since we seemed to have slipped into other identities. It was great fun! During that busy week, Ingolf and I each had obligations—he with his family and I with the last of the East Berliners whom I had committed myself to help. I had promised a woman in the West that I would go to her fiancé in East Berlin to get his power of attorney so she could withdraw savings from his West Berlin bank to use to buy goods that could be smuggled back to him by people like me. It was tricky business, because if I had been followed—which happened occasionally—and was caught with the document, we both would have been in big trouble.

However, when I got to his address he wasn't there—fortunately! On my way back into West Berlin, I was kept at Checkpoint Charlie for a long, long time, indicating that I had indeed been followed. I heard many muffled phone calls and recognized my name, but no one questioned me. I sat for a long time, grateful that I had never gotten the document. But I was soon supposed to meet Ingolf and his parents at the opera; I'm sure the East German guards already knew of my plans, because when I had crossed into East Berlin, they found my opera ticket when they searched me. Now, they were going to teach me a lesson—they were going to make sure that I didn't get to the opera on time.

Ingolf, of course, had no idea what had happened. His parents took their seats at the opera, but he stood in the back, in the standing-room section, waiting for me. His father Werner looked back, and saw him leaning against the wall, and later told him angrily, "A gentleman does not lean against a wall!" Ingolf, when he later told me this, was livid. This was the first indication I had that Werner, under his cordial exterior, could be a rather Old World tyrant, lacking sensitivity.

Ingolf never ever re-established a relationship with his father. He tried. And I would submit that one reason that Ingolf is so healthy now is because—this may sound harsh—his father was gone for so many years. I think if he hadn't been away, if he had been at home, that the family would have been screwed up. But when his father died, it was the first time I ever saw Ingolf cry. He was undone. That was the end. There would never be a chance for him to have a real relationship with his father.

By the time Mary Ellen and I finally boarded a plane for Cologne from Tempelhof Airport we were both exhausted. From Cologne, we took the night train to Paris, where we stayed in a pension near the Arc de Triomphe.

We then had a glorious day in Paris. Dinner was at the Rotisserie de la Pepigneire, a place Uncle Hugo had recommended. I even stole an ashtray to remember where we had been.

On our wedding day in Radnor, Pennsylvania.

Our flight to New York was the next day at noon. However, we overslept and got to Orly Airport late. The TWA clerk first told us that the flight was closed, then apparently took pity on us. I had my violin with me, and we must have looked innocent enough. She took us by the arms and rushed us through passport control onto the plane where they put us in first class—the only seats that were left.

It was our first transcontinental flight—in seats 2A and 2B—and I said to Mary Ellen, "When you travel with me, it will always be first class." I didn't have a penny to my name, but I felt that I had to impress her. Little did I know at that time that such things meant nothing to her. On September 8, we landed at Idlewild (now JFK) Airport.

We settled in near each other in Philadelphia, and Mary Ellen continued to work for the American Friends Service Committee while I began graduate school at Wharton. The MBA is normally a two-year program, but I managed to do it in one year plus two summer school sessions. I started in the fall of '62 at Wharton and finished all my course work, except for my thesis, by the following August so I could go back to work—because that August Mary Ellen and I were to be married. Our wedding day was August 17, 1963 (for numerologists: I was born 7/18/36, we were married 8/17/63). I finished my thesis the following summer and was able to graduate with the class of '64.

My life in America was about to begin "for real," and, thanks to Mary Ellen, what a life it would be.

NINE

FAST FORWARD:
THE CIRCLE IS COMPLETE

On November 9, 1989, twenty-eight years after I had left Berlin and Germany for good, East Germany officially opened the border between East and West Berlin. Thousands flocked to the checkpoints, and little by little the East Germans, together with West Germans, began demolishing the wall. The excitement throughout the world was palpable.

That same day, I got a call from my son. Eric said, "Pop, we have to go over to see this."

I have always been a believer in participating in history, to the extent I can, but that the initiative came from one of my children particularly motivated me. The very next day, the four of us—Mary Ellen and I, and our children, Eric and Ellen—flew over to Berlin. We arrived at the airport, rented a car, and stopped at a hardware store to buy a hammer and a chisel.

We drove to the northern portion of where West Berlin and East Berlin meet, to a place where the wall had been completely untouched. We started banging, and getting our pieces of the wall. Some of the West Berlin police came by and said, "Don't do that." They were nervous, I think because of the possible reaction from the East—that we still could have been shot. Everything was in a state of suspense.

We went farther south, and eventually got to the Brandenburg Gate. Here was the wall, and East German police standing on top of it—just standing there, looking down. Nothing was happening. They didn't know what to do.

There was a hole in the wall through which you could look into East Berlin. It was about a foot long and half a foot wide. Eric was taking pictures, and a smiling young East German policeman was looking through the wall from the other side.

It was really exciting. We couldn't believe it. *I* couldn't believe it. Then there came a point when a section of the wall was knocked down completely, and a street that once traversed the wall opened up. The East Germans poured into West Berlin, unimpeded—in cars and on foot. There was a West German band playing music. People were honking their horns. Everybody was slapping one another on the back.

I said to my family, "I want to ride with you on the ghost subway line." That was a line that started in West Berlin, went through four or five East Berlin stations, and then came back to West Berlin. That subway line operated even when the wall was up. When you passed through the East Berlin stations, they were dimly lit and you could see that they were barricaded. The trains didn't stop at them, but you could see the station signs.

When we boarded the train in West Berlin, it was almost empty. When we came to the first station in East Berlin, the train stopped. After nearly thirty years, it was the very first day that the trains made stops in the East since the wall had gone up. East Berliners piled in; many were going to West Berlin for the first time in their lives. A row of silent, pale, wide-eyed faces across the aisle stared at us—an American family. Only then did we notice that we did, indeed, look somewhat different. There were a few more stops, and then we were back in West Berlin. Everybody got out. It was amazing. We filmed it with a movie camera.

The fall of the Berlin Wall was a historic event. It signaled the end of the Soviet Union and almost forty-five years of the Iron Curtain. It set many millions of Central and East Europeans free. Berlin was an undivided city again— for the first time since I had been a small child. Even though I had now been an American for decades, I felt like a Berliner again that day.

The circle was complete.

Tearing down the Berlin Wall, with Mary Ellen and our son and daughter,
November 1989.

An East German policeman looking through a crack in the wall; photo taken by my
son, Eric.

EPILOGUE

None of us can escape our past, especially not the formative years of childhood and youth. My childhood was unconventional and sometimes tumultuous, but it does not compare to that of the millions of children who grow up every day without any hope, under atrocious conditions; who are killed, or starve to death.

My wife, Mary Ellen, with her Quaker breeding and Oregon background, gradually and patiently smoothed out some of the rough edges I had acquired during my "survival of the fittest" youth. We settled down, and I began what can reasonably be called a successful business career. On March 3, 1967, when I was thirty years old, I became a US citizen in a ceremony in the U.S. District Court in New Haven, Connecticut. We now have a vibrant family with two children—Ellen and Eric—and five grandchildren—Emily, Lily, Thomas, Elana, and Maxine. Both of our children married foreigners, in a sense stepping in their parents' footsteps. Ellen married James, an Englishman, and Eric married Heike, a German.

I love America with all my heart. Its diversity, "can do" attitude, and general optimism are unparalleled anywhere else in the world. When I first arrived here during the Eisenhower years, I was also deeply impressed by America's pragmatism in dealing with issues domestic and foreign. That pragmatism has faded recently, and ideology on the Far Right and Far Left has left the moderate middle of the population almost without a voice. But I am confident that saner voices will prevail again.

My background has taught me to be skeptical of extremists, be they political ideologues or religious fanatics present in all three Judeo-Christian religions. Adolf Hitler has shown us where it can lead if a charismatic ideologue takes over a whole country. I shudder at the expression of too much overt patriotism, flag waving, or talk of 'exceptionalism' of this or that country. I don't understand why Hollywood makes so many war movies when the reality of war has been and is horrible for mankind. I believe that hardly any of the people who make those movies or act in them have ever actually experienced war.

Still, I believe that the Constitution of the United States—and more than two hundred years of democracy—provide a barrier to extremism. Germany did not have that tradition when the Nazis took over, and even today its democracy is relatively young—less than thirty years in the former East Germany. When I go back to Germany—for family or business reasons, or for many years as a founding member of the American Academy in Berlin—I find a peaceful country that is integrated into the European Community. It counts Israel as one of its closest friends. Nevertheless, every time I land in Germany, I have a knot in my stomach. There are too many memories of the war years and the years that followed. I sometimes sense, in conversations with today's Germans, that the old resentments and prejudices against foreigners and Jews are still there, simmering just below the surface. I hope that I am wrong. But I would not choose to live in Germany again.

During my years at Duke University and the Wharton School, I was still very much a German student with a German mindset. Duke made my start in the US possible by providing me with a full-tuition scholarship. It was the first of many tangible examples I experienced of the generosity of the American spirit. I have tried to repay that kindness by volunteering for Duke and giving financial support, including for foreign students, ever since.

In Duke's archives, I first read and found out more about the Nazi atrocities than I had ever imagined. As I was reading about that, open racism still prevailed in the South, with segregation everywhere, including on my own campus. Eventually, though underlying prejudices continue to thrive, official segregation ended in America,

There are many stories told by people who have survived World War II. My story is one of a German child growing up under the Nazis and coming to America to learn the facts. It is different from other stories in that I was never persecuted by the Nazis because of race or opposition. I have struggled throughout my life with the realization that my father was a Nazi Party member and an officer in the Nazi army during World War II. I lived a life of relative privilege until it all came crashing down. Yet, in America, I was given the opportunity for a new life. For that I am forever grateful.

ABOUT THE AUTHOR

Karl M. von der Heyden was born in Berlin, Germany, in 1936, and made his way to America in 1957, upon receiving a full scholarship to study at Duke University. After graduating from Duke and obtaining an MBA degree from the Wharton School of the University of Pennsylvania, von der Heyden went on to become an accomplished corporate leader, serving as Chief Financial Officer, Chief Executive Officer, and Vice Chair of the Board at a variety of companies, including H.J. Heinz Company, PepsiCo, and RJR Nabisco. He is Chair Emeritus of the American Academy in Berlin where he was a founding trustee of the cultural institution in 1998. He lives in New York City, with his wife, Mary Ellen.